CH00656768

You've Got This! No Matter What!

How to Reinvent Your Life in 6 Steps

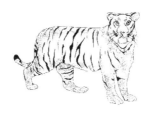

Valerie Dwyer

Best Seller Author and Award-Winning Entrepreneur

Published by My Wonderful Life Coach

www.mywonderfullifecoach.co.uk

info@mywonderfullifecoach.co.uk

ISBN: 978-1-8382055-1-5

DEDICATION

For my loving, supportive and inspirational family: Patrick, Bernie,
Gary, Lee, Caroline, Ellie, Ruby, Layton, Layla and Evie.

ACKNOWLEDGMENTS

Thank you especially to my family, to my friends, everyone who is and has been part of my journey. Far too many to name individually but you know who you are and I love and value you all.

Thank you to my mentors, coaches and clients, the key people who have inspired and motivated me to overcome challenges to develop the powerful, holistic and transformational Destination Me ™ programme around which this book is based, and get my message out into the world.

Paul Dunn, Chairman of B1G1; Roger J Hamilton, Founder of GeniusU, Entrepreneurs Institute, Entrepreneur Resorts, and other enterprises; Andy Harrington, Founder of Public Speakers University; Jack Black, Founder of Mindstore and Chris J Henry, ActionCOACH

Tom Peters, Brian Tracy, Tony Robbins, Paul McKenna

A very special Thank You to Ruth Sullivan and my fellow authors of Your Authority Book Group and The Rising Tide for their unwavering encouragement to Just Write It Already

FOREWORD BY PAUL DUNN

This is a book that changes lives.

In this case yours.

And what a privilege it is to be part of that journey you're on right now thanks to Valerie's superb book.

My 'role' here is to get you started — to get you ready for what's about to happen.

So, let me begin in an unconventional way. I want to start with a confession.

Now of course, it's unusual to start a foreword to a great, wonderful, inspiring book with a confession.

So, since I like doing things just a little differently, let me start with not one confession but two. Here we go:

Confession 1: I love music. Music moves me.

Confession 2: I love most things Apple.

And those things came together for me early in the morning here in Singapore on 12th September 2017.

Because of confession 2, I was sitting at my computer (yes, it's a Mac) at 20 minutes before midnight waiting for the launch of a new Apple product — the iPhone X.

As with everything Apple does, the event was perfectly curated. And that was particularly true of the music streaming that day. Just a super 'mix'. Then on came a song about 3 minutes before Apple's

CEO Tim Cook took the stage… I'd NEVER heard it before. And what a perfect song it was.

But since I didn't have my phone with me, I couldn't pop on Shazam and find out what the song was.

So later on I typed into Google — 'songs played at launch of iPhone X'. And there was the whole playlist. And there was that perfect song.

And it's perfect for now as you open your body, your heart and your soul to Valerie's words.

The song is by Imagine Dragons. Here's the chorus:

Whatever it takes

'Cause I love the adrenaline in my veins

I do whatever it takes

'Cause I love how it feels when I break the chains

Whatever it takes

Yeah, take me to the top

I'm ready for whatever it takes

'Cause I love the adrenaline in my veins

I do what it takes

That's you. Doing whatever it takes.

Whatever it takes to live a life that's totally full of wonderment.

Whatever it takes to find your very own North Star; that special something that you know is bigger than you that you were put here to do.

That special something that makes your heart (and mine when I meet you) truly sing.

That special something that leads you not just to make a difference in your life but then leads you to share that with others. You don't just leave a legacy. Your live it each moment. And you leverage it by inspiring others each moment too.

That's you doing whatever it takes. Not to put on climbing equipment and oxygen bottles to climb the highest mountains. But simply to do whatever it takes to be fully open to your time with Valerie.

And then to find that special something that's wrapped up so beautifully in you.

That's simply got to be the best thing happening in your world and in ours right this moment.

Do whatever it takes to lean in, to learn, to be curious, to explore, to wonder.

And imagine no more.
It's right here. Right now.
Paul Dunn, Chairman B1G1

Paul Dunn is a 4 times TEDx speaker. He was one of the first 10 people in Hewlett Packard in Australia, he started one of Australia's first computer companies and he founded The Results Corporation, working with and developing over 23,000 businesses.

Paul has been honoured as a Social Innovation Fellow in his new home of Singapore.

He rocked the Accounting Profession through his radical

Accountants' Boot Camp where he helped over 17,000 Accountants found new ways to work with clients.

Paul has been featured in Forbes Magazine with Sir Richard Branson as a 'disrupter' in business. And even though he's not an Accountant, he became the first person ever to receive Accounting Web's "Outstanding Contribution to the Profession" award.

His seminal books include "The Firm of The Future" (co-authored with Ron Baker), which is widely regarded as one of the most important of its type ever written.

Paul's unique Business Development programs are now in use by an estimated 226,000 companies around the world.

He now serves as the Chairman of the revolutionary B1G1, enabling businesses to connect and give back in new ways and creating over 205 Million giving impacts globally.

You've Got This!

No Matter What!

A NOTE ON FORTUOSITY!

I had the good fortune to meet two people who encouraged me to achieve two major goals from my own Vision, while taking part in an Entrepreneurs Institute Programme in Bali, after a winning entry in the Global Impact Award for Women Entrepreneurs Making a Difference in the World.

Roger J Hamilton, Founder of Entrepreneurs Institute, of which I am a member, really understood my ambition to take the Destination Me™ Intensive programme from one-to-one working with VIP entrepreneurs to one-to-many globally and suggested I develop and formalise the structure so that other trained Entrepreneurs, Coaches, Consultants will be able to facilitate and deliver it. I set this goal then and this is now on the way to being achieved with the imminent online launch.

Paul Dunn, Chairman of B1G1 Business For Good, the Global Giving Initiative, introduced me to the Power of Small and how we all can make a BIG difference and powerful impacts by compounding small acts of giving. Paul also encouraged me to get clear on my Why? and to achieve the programme goal plus get on and write this book.

With every experience, you alone are painting your   own canvas, thought by thought, choice by choice."

Oprah Winfrey

CONTENTS

COURAGE! Change is the ONLY Way to Be, Do, Have More! Lead That Change Yourself!
Never, Ever Give Up On Your Dreams!

Valerie Dwyer

Advance reviews…

"**A transformational book that inspires you to review & renew your life goals!** Valerie has created something special that helps you achieve your goals in a practical and refreshing way. You've got to get this book... now! Highly recommended."
Liam O'Connell, Speaker/Consultant/Author

"**I have read many books over the years but none that gave me the insights and transformational change as 'You've Got This, No Matter What'.** This book will lead you on a journey of self-discovery like no other. I have known Valerie for many years and have seen first-hand the transformation she has achieved for her clients. Valerie has now taken her work and her wisdom and is sharing it with the world in this fabulous, thought-provoking, practical and transformational book. From the personal stories to the guided exercises, this is a journey into the power of the mind and the opportunity that each and every one of us has to make the changes to ourselves and our lives that we desire."
Mel Colling, Director and Founder, Purpose Driven Projects and Experts on Air

"This book is the definitive most comprehensive, logical, structured approach to establishing your Purpose in life, your Why? your Vision.

The book gives an insight into the interactive programme created by Valerie Dwyer, My Wonderful Life Coach™ which, having been through it, I can highly recommend. Anyone with any doubts look at Valerie's impressive track record, read this book and then engage yourself in a life changing opportunity by booking on the amazing Destination Me™ Programme... Clarity X Action = Results."

Chris Henry, Business & Wealth Coach, MindYerWealth Ltd

"**Fantastic book!** Valerie has certainly captured all the tools of self-agency and put them into a usable and practical process guide for someone to follow. This book certainly reinforces, even for the experienced entrepreneur, the necessity to continually put these techniques into practice whenever there is self-doubt or when things aren't going the way you want them to. Motivational."

Neil Marwick, Co-founder and Director, MIWorld Network

Powerful Words to think about before we begin….

"Our deepest fear is not that we are inadequate. Our deepest fear is that we are powerful beyond measure. It is our light, not our darkness that most frightens us. We ask ourselves, 'Who am I to be brilliant, gorgeous, talented, fabulous?'

Actually, who are you not to be? You are a child of God. Your playing small does not serve the world. There is nothing enlightened about shrinking so that other people won't feel insecure around you. We are all meant to shine, as children do.

We were born to make manifest the glory of God that is within us. It's not just in some of us; it's in everyone. And as we let our own light shine, we unconsciously give other people permission to do the same. As we are liberated from our own fear, our presence automatically liberates others."

Marianne Williamson

INTRODUCTION

YOU are already Amazing! By the virtue of being alive, being here, and with the curiosity to explore a truly life changing opportunity right now for you.

The intention behind this book is to EMPOWER YOU! To help you go inside yourself and see how wonderful you are. To endow your ability to create your own Vital Vision Blueprint™, the firm foundation for your new life and for getting through whatever life throws at you!

Why write this book? Because I have a Belief and a Vision to share that changed my life and the lives of thousands of other entrepreneurs and it can change your life too!

You see I believe that by each one of us reconnecting with our own Inner Vision Compass, birthing our Vision for Good out into the world through our Vital Vision™ Blueprint, living our legacy and sharing it, we are creating a Wonderful World at the same time as we create our Wonderful Lives.

I believe:

When You Have A Powerful, Exciting and Crystal-Clear Vision For How You Can Create Your Life And Your World, Everything Changes. And THAT'S When the Magic! Happens!

You see, when your life hangs by a thread, as mine has done, suddenly everything comes sharply into FOCUS!

This Vision grew and, as it did so, saved my life! More than once! In the process I discovered how wonderful life can be. Now my mission is to save other lives, including yours by sharing the gifts I have been granted and also giving back, in gratitude for my life.

This is one reason why we are a When Good…Then Good…. Business. When something good happens in our business we gift something good into the world and our clients make this happen.

I'll explain a little more, but first…

I want to ask you a question.

If you could stop now and take the time out to design and create the life you REALLY want, would you, if you knew how? Well, this is the opportunity that I am about to share right now with you!

As a 'Creative' I love to 'fly' metaphorically speaking that is, to 'see' the bigger picture! But it's also necessary to be able to ground myself to take roots in a firm foundation from time to time. This is the balance. Like Ying and Yang, Up and Down, Backwards and Forwards, everything connects and has an equal and exact opposite.

Flexibility is essential in times of crisis and chaos, to be able to deal with survival practicalities while also opening your inner eye and inner vision to how you will be and what you will do when this time passes.

If you had the chance to create not only a 'new normal' but a 'better normal' in the world, why wouldn't you?

Destination Me™ Intensive, around which this book is based, is delivered by My Wonderful Life Coach™, founded to help create a Wonderful World. A Wonderful Sustainable World for everyone who joins us as they are then in turn are creating a Wonderful World for all of us, and on a much bigger scale.

As you will read, we take further practical live action in this direction through our lifetime global partnership with B1G1 Business For Good, the global giving initiative, changing lives every day, just by doing what we do!

Having experienced being 'lost' in my life several times in the distant past, before I truly found my Self, surviving significant emotional events and experiences, economic downturns, recessions, this flexibility, the ability to reinvent, creating ten businesses on the journey, is second nature to me. If there were a Masters in Resilience and Bounce Back Ability, I'm certain I have qualified.

Every lesson in this book is a real lesson that I have not only learned, but experienced, through the intervention of the Universe (so not always pleasant) but built my resilience and courage that saved me and my life in one way or another, and I wish the same for you.

This book gives you the powerful foundation you need to overcome any wobble but you will need to persevere with every exercise to enjoy the benefits. Do the work and you'll find this is a powerful piece of work, not simply an interesting read.

My sincere hope is this. That the process I have developed from breaking through barriers and crushing challenges, that thousands of entrepreneurs have now learned the secrets of to turn their lives around from stuck to success, will help you too.

I'll share with you the 6 powerful, tried and proven steps that have helped empower thousands of entrepreneurs to get through challenges and chaos, from stuck to success as they reinvented their lives and businesses. And will do this for you too!

Many of these entrepreneurs could not see their own potential, did not know they had an amazing Inner Vision waiting to be born, had unfulfilled dreams and in some cases had no dream at all. Some knew what they didn't want but had no idea what they really wanted, or what their next step should be!

In all cases, working through this programme was what gave them clarity, direction and focus, but more importantly revealed to them their BIG VISION for their life, their True Purpose that, once it is clear, pulls you forward in to Flow, rather than being pushed by the pain of recurring problems.

In sharing some of my story I searched for what will help explain how I developed the elements of Destination Me™ that will enable you to reinvent and reset yourself to the you, you were born to be.

The resilient, resourceful human being that you are, knowing and living your time and purpose in life with ease, confidence and success in whoever you discover you really are while working through this book with me.

Probably the most profound part of my own journey is that, eventually, I learned the ability to step outside of any situation, especially those which were or are highly emotional, and become the observer.

As the observer, detached from the emotions we have the choice - to engage with those emotions or not.

This discovery, and the opportunity to go back into those most powerful experiences, enabled me to crack the code to creating positive IMPACTful and life changing experiences for others.

Being able to step out and analyse the circumstances of each event, and what made them so powerful, memorable and impactful on my life, I was able to harness those elements and incorporate them.

This means that this experiential process, and the Vital Vision™ Blueprint session in particular that I share, connects with your feelings and emotions to be anchored and embedded as a powerful and positive memory in your subconscious.

Unlike any Vision Board made from clippings from magazines or other papers therefore, your vision becomes a living part of you.

In a similar way that skilled habitual activities, such as driving a car or riding a bike, are run automatically by programmes in our subconscious, achievement of your Vision when you have worked through this process becomes natural.

Even when you are not consciously thinking about it, your subconscious will be looking for opportunities 24/7 and 365 to make it happen! But remember, just as you had to practise to learn to drive and pass your test and as you had to practise without stabilisers to learn to ride a bicycle, you have to do the work to get to this stage! And no one else can do this for you!

We'll be getting down to some basics so that you have all the steps you need. Stick with it and go through the book chapter by chapter and do the work in sequence. Don't be tempted to skip and miss anything out, even if you think you already know some of it, which you may well do.

At the core of your reinvention is your Inner Vision Compass. We reconnect to your Inner Vision Compass to birth your Vital Vision™ Blueprint out into the world to enable it to become reality. There are however, critical steps that you need to take both before and after this process.

There is much you may not consciously know about yourself. It is all relevant to taking you on this journey of discovery now, to finding yourself, designing the life you really want and beginning to live it by the end of this book!

More about When Good…Then Good…

When something Good happens in our business, this triggers us to gift something Good into the world. For example, through our lifetime global partnership with B1G1, when someone buys one of our books, we gift education and reading materials to children.

For buying this book you have already begun to contribute. Here is what you have caused to happen:

- ♥ You have funded training for new entrepreneurs in less fortunate countries.
- ♥ You have given access to education and reading materials for young girls who otherwise would have none.
- ♥ You have provided fresh, life-saving water for families who need it.
- ♥ You have planted fruit trees that serve as shelters for wildlife, sources of income for poor families and help to purify the air we breathe, reduce pollution and improve our environment.

All through the Lifetime Global Partnership of B1G1 Business For Good and My Wonderful Life Coach™.

Thank you again for buying and more importantly, reading.

You Did This! Thank you!

When you reach the Case Study at the end - and don't immediately rush there - you will have the opportunity to give something even more astounding……

You were born to lead a Wonderful Life. So come on. Let's move on!

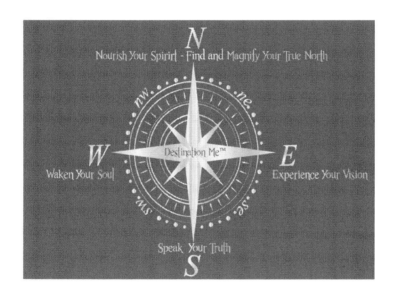

First, Think. Second, Dream. Third, Believe.

And finally, Dare

Walt Disney

The Process

This is what Roger J Hamilton, Futurist and Founder of GeniusU, Entrepreneurs Institute, Entrepreneur Resorts and other enterprises had to say when we talked about Vision during an Entrepreneurs Institute iLab session in Bali…. In his exact words….

"Hands up whoever heard of this idea of creating a vision board. Okay why is it that it often doesn't work at the level we think it would work?

Well, Valerie has figured it out! And she actually has a proven product called Destination Me™ which has at the heart of it something which is called her Vision Compass™. Powerful because the Vision Compass gives you a really, really, clear direction way beyond the picture of your vision itself.

And if you think of a Compass, it kind of looks like this and it's got a big arrow and the first thing she does is she ..

The first step in the process is - Nourish your Spirit

And what this means is she'll put you into an environment where you have music, movement, colour; where you have images but also inputs so you get inspired. Spirit means Breath, so you are actually in a meditative state, tapping into where it is you are going. Most people don't get into that state but we have got all these tools and once you allow this to happen you actually get into that space.

Step Two - Experience Your Vision

When this is where you go into this whole experience of where you're sharing it, to yourself first of all, where you're putting yourself in a really beautiful place, a Beach Club, a Retreat, but you can do it in your own home, creating this beautiful place where you internalise, then externalise, writing down, seeing what you're feeling. You're seeing why you love this, more than this, at the same time, you are **Wakening Your Soul**

Step Three - Wakening Your Soul

You're shutting down your mind and your Inner Critic so you are not allowed to speak, not allowed to be thinking things through from a logical point of view and saying why it can't happen, not listening to your small voice inside-so there are techniques we use so you can be apart from that. So, you are shutting down your thoughts in a way that your Soul is actually opening and wakens so you've experienced your vision, wakened your Soul and that's when the **Power** then comes in. You then get to **Speak Your Truth.**

Step Four - Speak Your Truth

Speak your truth and you are speaking your truth to others who have already gone through the same process so they are already open to that as well, and then you co-create a future that is your future and their future as well". And you remember this because the **N for Nourish your Spirit** and the **E for Experience your Vision** and the **S for**

Speak Your Truth and the **W for Wakening Your Soul** give you your **Compass** - which then allows you to know your place, where you are heading and find your **True North**."

The 12 Rules

1. YOU are in Charge of YOU

2. Do What It Takes! With What You Have

3. Take Your Time

4. Read the Appendices First

5. Gather Your Materials and Resources

6. Create Your Space

7. Give Yourself Permission

8. Meditate or Learn to Meditate and do before each Exercise

(FREE training details in Master Your Mindful Meditation)

9. Do every exercise and Stick With It to the End

10. Ask Me Any Questions

11. Share Your Feedback

12. Rate this Book!

Sometimes Daring to Do What You Fear To Do, Is the ONLY Thing That Will Get You Through!

6 STEPS TO REINVENT YOUR LIFE!

Chapter One

WHO ARE YOU REALLY?

"Cherish your Visions and Your Dreams as They are the Children of Your Soul, the Blueprints of your Ultimate Achievements"

Napoleon Hill

Are you living to anything like your full potential? If you dared to dream, who would you become?

Before we begin, I want to thank you for being here. I am delighted because you are about to discover the Most Important Work you can ever do for you, beginning today.

If you are here because you want to change your life, whether in a small or very BIG way, then you are in the right place.

For best effect, schedule yourself some 'me time', clear your calendar, take yourself to a quiet place, check the environment requirements in the appendices, gather the materials also listed there, and begin with the intention of going inside yourself and working on the Inner You.

To bring out your true Inner Vision and Purpose by working mindfully through each exercise, the 6 Steps to Success of Destination Me™ detailed in this book. And above all, allow yourself to imagine, to dream…

When you read through chapter by chapter, this book has a big and valid claim. The programme, extracted from Destination Me™, has changed thousands of lives for better.

People, both ambitious and already successful entrepreneurs and business owners, as well as struggling start-ups and self-doubters, have grown or spun off new businesses, founded national charities, written and published best-selling books in 30 days, won major Awards, taken their speaking business onto global stages, launched their own online programmes and much more over the 20 years it has been running.

You now have the secrets it contains to overcoming chaos and crisis in your life at any time. Getting rid of doubt and procrastination. Stopping self-sabotage. Reinventing yourself from the inside out!

My own experience covers 30 years building 10 businesses, several recessions, economic boom and bust and personal life events and crises that enabled me to shape this experience into knowledge and a system that has helped thousands of people get back up, even from rock bottom!

If you are stuck or blocked or caught in or affected by chaos or crisis the great news is that you have all you need within you right now to work your way through, and I want to show you how. With the knowledge in this book you can reinvent, recreate and revive yourself to survive and thrive.

This requires you to trust yourself and the process I will reveal through this book. Take all the time you need. It is different for everyone. What is important is that you read and work through every element, in the order shown, completing the exercises in order and continue through right to the end.

What could be more important for you than finding the way, the firm foundation for your life, a life that you love, that will set you on purpose with who you really are and enable you to be, do and have the life of your dreams?

What is wonderful is that once learned, these steps are in your life forever and can be repeated when the right time comes again.

There are exercises to do and you will need to set up the right environment for these to be most effective. You will also need some materials, but most should be to hand.

These are covered in your Checklists and Materials and Resources lists in the Appendices. You will also find it useful to keep a pen and jotter or journal handy to jot down any notes, or write them in this book, it's your choice.

Begin by setting your intention for this book. Make your commitment. Write it down.

"I commit to fully engage with the content of this book so that I will have the firm foundation to change my life for better".

Or choose your own words...

Come back to this commitment after you have read through the book to the last page AND done the work and reflect on what has changed for you.

Today is the first day of the rest of your life. Make it the best of your life.

Are you the person today that, as a child, you dreamed you would become?

If you are not happy with your life or business, decide right here and now to change it and come with me on a journey to your true self and the life you were born to lead…

You are whoever you think you are. Would it be easy or difficult for you to accept that your reality is the result of your thoughts? And that thoughts become things.

Thinking of this, what story are you now telling yourself and the world about you? Is it one that builds you up and serves you or one that pulls you back into a reality you would love to escape? Only you know the truth!

You are more powerful than you may ever know, until faced with your greatest challenge!

Having been in that situation many times, I speak from experience!

You have done the Outer Work, many times over no doubt. Now, you are ready for change or you would not be here. Only you can change you, so it is time to do your Inner Work and that takes a willingness to explore, try new things and that takes courage!

So, muster up your courage now. Remember,

"Change is the ONLY way to be, do, have more. Lead that change for yourself and never, ever give up on your Dreams!"

If you dared to dream now, who could you, would you become? This work is not difficult but may well be challenging, because this book is all about YOU!

Did you ever think or wish you were living a different life? Ever ask yourself how on earth you came to be living the life the way you have and now do? Have you ever attempted to change before in a big way?

Here's the brilliant news! If you are not happy, you always have choices.

Continue as you are or do something different.

Change or don't change.

I'm guessing that because you are here reading this, you want something more than you've had before, whatever that may be, even though you may not yet know what this is.

You will know by the end of this book!

In times of personal challenge or difficulty, crisis or chaos, when we feel extremely unsettled, we are being sent a nudge to change.

Perhaps a gentle tap? When we don't take action, Universe steps in and makes that message a whack around the head, louder and clearer, so that we have no alternative but to change.

In fact the change happens, in spite of us.

Unfortunately, the message is not always delivered pleasantly but is an extreme wake-up call, as I know only too well!

Now and again a global situation takes place that pulls us all in. It brings the precious gift of time and space that in our busy, busy lives we ourselves were not prepared to give, to pause or stop and do some deep thinking and re-connecting and re-aligning with our true selves.

When we take notice we get to see where we were off track in order to come back on our course, or if our course was unclear, to guide us into what we need to do next.

It is only natural to fear a time to go within, such as this, because it will lead inevitably to reconnecting with our feelings, emotions and to perhaps making some tough decisions.

Stick with me. I know how uncomfortable it is to step out of your Comfort Zone in order to go for what you really want, the life of your dreams! You may need to become your Courage Tiger.

Been there, done that, got several t-shirts and my choices were often not voluntary as you'll discover through the book when I share lessons learned that have helped me discover how to help myself - and you.

Better news is that when you choose the change option and work through this book in sequence, doing each exercise to the best of your ability, by the end you will have not only learned the secret to your transformation but it will already have had a positive impact on you.

That's a bold statement I know but I also know it to be true from the feedback of the thousands of people, mostly entrepreneurs (because that's a label I also attracted) already helped. Got any labels yourself?

Sometime later, much later, and some really difficult experiences, I learned all of the lessons I am now able to share with you. Years, well decades in fact that finally led me to my true purpose. That is to share the result of going through my experiences of 'overcoming' and 'reinventing' in order to help you.

A little bit about me.... Born in Yorkshire, UK, at a time of rationing, and growing up in a small Lincolnshire village, I learned to be careful with everything!

My grandmother's sayings still ring in my head today. The conditioning that I had no idea at the time was happening to me and shaping my life. "A little bit of egg and a big bit of bread" at breakfast when we were not having porridge.

Even though Gran was nearly fully self-sufficient and hatched her own chickens from eggs laid carefully on a towel, placed over a tray in the still warm oven of the old black iron coal fired kitchen range, food and other resources were scarce, so she sold the eggs for income. I loved to hear the newborns cheeping and to hold those warm and fluffy chicks.

When we sat at the fireside on winter evenings, darning holes in clothes, or making rag rugs from cut up old garments past their best, she would say "A stitch in time saves nine" or "Make do and mend".

By the age of 5 she had taught me to skin a rabbit, dissect a chicken, and learn what happened to the pig I used to love talking to and feeding with a pail of 'swill' twice a day.

Gran was truly an entrepreneur, although that description did not exist then. She taught me how to make something out of nothing so that when in later life recessions or 'boom and bust' came and went I was fully prepared.

Fortunately, my childhood experiences did equip me with my Gran's resourcefulness, but absolutely nothing for dealing with the emotional mayhem that came from the experiences sent to teach me those lessons. I had to learn these for myself! It's the unexpected though that we've never had to deal with before that swerves us off course.

And much later I discovered that these were in fact gifts for sharing. I hope these help you too.

Let's begin to explore who you are and what you love. Do the following exercises that will give some clues!

Exercise 1:

What story are you currently telling yourself and others about you? Don't overthink this or make it up as you go along. Be honest and write it out quickly.

_____

_____

_____

_____

_____

Is this Story True?

_____

_____

_____

Exercise 2:

Now, what do you absolutely love about you? Come on, don't be shy! Think about Who you are, your character, talents, moments of joy, achievements, celebrations, successes. What do other people love about you? Feel free....

Exercise 3.

Now how do you feel about the story you have been telling yourself and others? If it was true - that's wonderful!

If not, what story would you LOVE to be telling yourself and others about you? Write the story you love here and commit to living it forward....

Exercise 4.

What is the most significant thing you learned from this chapter?

'Why Am I here? Why Am I Not?

I Knew as A Child, then Grew Up and Forgot

Chapter Two

WHY ARE YOU?

D o you know that one of the most common questions in the world is Why Am I Here? It certainly is in my experience!

Every life has a purpose. It is the reason we are born. The trouble is that we don't come with an Instruction Book and not everyone is already tuned in, like a radio, to their right frequency.

We were so close to our purpose as children because life was an adventure with everything to be explored. Then we learned the ways of the world and were taught how to conform.

So often it is only after many years of life experiences that people either see a pattern emerge for what they love and want to be doing for the rest of their life or the Universe gives them a nudge, which they ignore, then they get a tap on the shoulder and, if the message is still ignored, there comes a great big whack around the head! Oh! Boy do I know that!

Been there, done that and admit to having several t-shirts! But thankfully, each event had messages that brought me to where I am today.

Sharing what I have learned from overcoming major challenges, significant emotional events and life-changing experiences how to create an impactful process that transforms people's lives and helps them create a better world at the same time.

My question to you is "Could you Be More You?" if you knew why you are you?

Sounds like a puzzle doesn't it, much of life is until you figure it out!

Yes, really. Why are you here living this life in the way you are? Is it through free will or have you been conditioned or shoe-horned into living the life that others expect of you, or at least the one you think they expect?

An accident, you might feel or think? Everything that is or ever existed was for a purpose and you are no exception. Have you ever thought about this? Have you discovered your life's Purpose yet?

Do you ever just go through the motions and habitual e-motions day to day? Same repetition? Looking forward to the end of the working day? Or the weekend? Hoping for something to turn up?

Are you pushed by pain or pulled by a powerful purpose that gets you so excited you are jumping out of bed every morning to get on with your wonderful life?

Brilliant news! When you have worked through to the end of this book, page by page, chapter by chapter, in the order as written AND do ALL the exercises in the same order, you will be much clearer on both who you are and why you are here. Not only this, but you will also know exactly where you are going from now forward. Into the life that YOU have designed.

Then your decision will simply be whether to Go For It! To live the life you were born to lead, or not! Your life of flow, harmony and abundance, lived confidently, knowing that you are on exactly the right path for you!

Be warned though, as you find out for the first time, or rediscover who you really are and why you are here on Planet Earth, this can feel frightening or threatening for those closest to you.

These feelings come from fear, perhaps fear of change, or fear of losing you. There are lots of reasons. I am sincerely hoping that having got your hands on a copy of this book, (and I don't believe in coincidences, things are meant to be because we attract them, which means you were meant to read and act upon it) you are curious enough to find out more and excited enough as we go forward to work all the way through.

I hope that people will be happy for you being on this journey you have chosen but let's be real, it is not always the case.

You have two choices. Tell them or don't tell them. You decide. Whatever you decide, somewhere along the way, they will notice a difference in you!

Knowing and voicing your WHY is SO powerful! We are aiming to arrive at your WHY? throughout this journey, in the context of your present and your future. In a way that you can encapsulate it into a short paragraph so that you can easily remind yourself as well as share it with whomever needs to know. You will also find that you attract like-minded people, your 'tribe' as well as relevant opportunities to live your Why?

Your WHY? does not need to you to overthink it. It is within you. You FEEL it! It compels you to do the work you WANT to do. Regardless of obstacles and challenges you still feel driven to pursue your WHY? because it gives your life meaning. Other people on the same journey will be drawn to you too. In business, this is a definite advantage!

Everyone has a deep motivation that energises them and their life when they connect with it. You leave visible clues in who you are and what you do. It may be though that these are more apparent to those around you than to yourself.

So a good idea, if you are struggling with identifying your Why? is to ask yourself some questions and keep on asking until it becomes clear, until you SEE your Why? Remember, there are clues.

For example:

- Why do I do what I do?
- Why do I value this activity over that activity?
- Why do I get up every day?

One way you can express your Why? is in a sentence such as:

"I get up every morning to..................so that......

'That' being the outcome of who or what is positively impacted by what you do each day..

Daily reflection and journaling can signal if you are on the right track. When you feel fulfilled and in flow you are aligned with your Why? When you feel unfulfilled, unhappy it's a signal that something is out of sync.

- Check in daily for 5 minutes of reflection at the end of your day

- How happy, in flow and fulfilled did you feel in a scale of 1-10?

- What factors affected your score?

- What, if anything, do you need to do about this?

Check out the Why's of three or four leaders you follow or respect. Think about their Why? Statements. Don't copy but discover, then learn how to craft your own once you are clear on what your Why? is.

Start with Why? is a book by Simon Sinek that I highly recommend for gaining more insight into your own Why?

Complete the following exercises to help you along.

Exercise 1:

Now let's look for some clues! Look back. Think about your childhood. Take your time

What are things you loved to do that gave you happiness, joy and made you feel really good? List them all on a separate sheet of paper. Then bring your Top Three here and say why they made you feel this way:

1.

_____

_____

_____

2.

_____

_____

_____

3.

_____

_____

Exercise 2.

Now look to the more recent present, in the past year or so.

What are things you now love to do that give you happiness, fulfilment, joy and make you feel really good? List them all on a separate sheet of paper. Then bring your Top Three here and say why they make you feel this way:

1.

2.

3.

Exercise 3.

Now, what from all of these things you are capable of doing, what Top Three would you love to do from now forward, even if there is no external recognition and no financial return for doing them:

1.

_____

_____

_____

2.

_____

_____

3.

_____

_____

_____

Exercise 4:

Look forward in time. Now IMAGINE! What are things you have never attempted but always wanted to, and would still love to explore? What if you had only one week left to do ALL you still want to do? Write yourself your 'Bucket List' on a separate sheet of paper and add to it whenever you wish. Write your Top Three choices here and think what do they tell you about your Why? Say how you will fit them into your life!

1.

2.

3.

GREAT PROGRESS!

You are still in preparation though. After you have worked through the exercise in Chapter Eight this preparation will have served you well! But DO NOT rush there now, there's more powerful discovery awaiting you on this journey!

"Today is the First Day of the Rest of YOUR Life.

YOU Alone Have the Power to Make it the Best of Your Life"

Chapter Three

READY FOR A NEW YOU?

You are already Amazing! So, what or who would A New You look like?

Let's be positive. Imagine. What WILL the New You look like? Who would you absolutely love to be?

What superpower, skill or natural talent would you love to be using? And why?

Unsure? Then don't be. You have the power of IMAGINATION! To dream or daydream. You have the ability to visualise? Everyone has.

Don't think so? OK. What is the colour of your front door? Didn't you almost immediately see an image of your door or the colour of it? Let's try another. Where is the lock on your front door? See it now.

If you close your eyes, you can imagine your hands, so you have the power.

Not doing it for you? OK, let's attach some emotion!

Come into this image with me. Imagine! It's your holiday. You are sitting on a bleached sandy beach. There is music playing from somewhere behind you. It's a lovely sunny day, you can feel the heat rising up your arms as you watch the foaming white waves rolling in, the wind gently blowing your hair. You take off your dark sunglasses and pick up your book. Did you see that?

Believe in your power to visualise!

In my workshops I used to take attendees through my Lemon Exercise after a short meditation. It ends with everyone having seen, felt and tasted a sour lemon even to the extent that their mouths watered. There was no real lemon involved. All imagination.

Go on. Try it for yourself! With or without a meditation first. Imagine seeing and picking up that lemon from the kitchen table, feeling the solid dimpled texture of its oval shaped outer skin in your hands. See yourself put the lemon back on the table and cut it into two with a knife. Imagine yourself take half the lemon and suck the juice from it. What is your experience?

You may have heard marketers say: "Sell the sizzle, not the sausage" and this is the technique they use to get people attracted to try their products, especially food, but other products too!

Everything new for you starts in your imagination, as a picture, or like a video or a thought. Every new thing starts as an imagined idea to become a firm thought and thoughts then become things when we take action and pursue them to a conclusion. You really are the ultimate creator!

The very first tool, car, plane, telephone, television, all were imagined or dreamed before becoming firm thoughts which were then developed into drawings or blueprints and either created by the inventor or passed to engineers and craftsmen to produce.

You will learn the steps in this book for how to prepare the right environment conditions and the exact processes to go through in order to imagine, dream or visualise the life you want, turn it into a Blueprint, develop your strategies and masterplan for A New You and start living your new life, the life you absolutely love.

Sounds simple doesn't it?

This extremely powerful, effective and successful method of creating the New You that I am about to share with you involves so much more than this, though. Because you are not an inanimate thing or product.

You are a living, breathing human being with thoughts, feeling, emotions as well as ideas. Your own feelings and emotions can side-track you, in the same way that other people can put you off.

Sabotage and self-sabotage are equal pests in the garden of your life. You will overcome them by being resilient, resourceful and determined to follow through.

Have confidence though that I have thought about this many times, and refined the programme the more people I have worked with; even though they had amazing experiences and huge successes, I am always looking for how I can improve on what you are about to learn.

Have confidence and believe.

You CAN do this! Be brave and prepared to step out of your Comfort Zone if need be. Relax in the knowledge that you are on a tried, tested, proven and successful pathway.

You are about to reconnect with your Inner Vision and bring it out into the world in your Vital Vision™ Blueprint while experiencing the aligning your Heart, Mind, Body and Spirit. Everything will be OK! It's all right and it's all good.

You've Got This! No Matter What!

You can be whoever you decide you are going to be! This is the journey you are now on. But first, you need to know more about who the new you looks like.

Let's get you over your first hurdle, to Motivate Your Mindset!

"Your mind is your garden, your thoughts are your seeds, you can grow flowers or you can grow weeds"

Unknown

Chapter Four

STEP 1 MOTIVATE YOUR MINDSET

"You'll See It When You Believe It"

Dr Wayne Dyer

L et me share a little story that demonstrates the power of having a belief, combined with the right mindset to get you unstuck….

An unexpected intervention came about by a series of small coincidences! No, I don't believe in coincidence- this was meant to be. It served, and continues to serve my purpose…

One day I overheard something while walking past a television. At the time I was searching for support. I heard the words mindset and belief and turned to listen.

Someone called Jack Black was being interviewed on a business programme and at the end of his talk I heard the name 'Mindstore'.

This happened at a time I was so busy, and had become so stressed, that I was not stopping to use the trusted techniques I already knew. For the time being I thought no more of it and carried on, as we sometimes do!

A few months later, what should pop into sight but a newspaper article announcing Jack Black's 3 Day Mindstore event coming to my home town! At the time funds were stretched, but I knew at once that

I had to go.

With the event at a local hotel I would not need accommodation costs.

I also knew that with extra work the investment could be recovered, so I turned up on the first day still not quite sure what to expect.

To say I was blown away by what I learned is really an understatement. Payment for the whole three days was worth it for all that I learned but there were TWO POWERFUL THINGS that on their own were worth the money and more!

After a meditation Jack first took us through a live demonstration that showed us, linked to work on our mindset, the effect of drinking alcohol on our physical strength.

This was eye opening and I still credit Jack that I stopped drinking alcohol, tea, and coffee that day (despite having withdrawal symptoms for the next two days of the course!) and I stayed off for three years.

When I did return to these beverages it was by personal choice and decision. And I know that I can do this again, any time I want to, or indeed use the same technique for anything else I want to change.

However, that was not all. Jack proceeded to take us through an amazing exercise where I was able to build my 'House on the Right Bank' through a meditation, a mindset mechanism, a visualising process, for connecting a clear, short, quick pathway from my left Logic Brain into my right Creative Brain in a way that I could help other people create easy access too, in my programmes!

My Creative Brain has always been engaged, so for me it has been easy to have a vision and to visualise what I want, (some times easier than others, especially when my life had been impacted by extreme external circumstances). This tool though, this gift from Jack, gave me a structure to work with and I am forever grateful.

This works best in Theta State, (States are explained in the next chapter) so just before sleep is excellent. I have adapted the model over time and recorded my own version of this powerful process for creating a virtual representation of something tangible that you want and attracting it to you.

Let's look a little closer now...

Mindset - Oxford Concise English Dictionary

Habitual way of thinking.

Well, Good News! You can change your habits. It may take a couple of weeks, (well science says 21 days to be exact), but you can do it!

Mindset is Everything! Thoughts become things!

The word *mindset* was *first* used in the 1930's to mean "habits of *mind* formed by previous experience." In simple terms, *mindsets* are deeply held *beliefs*, attitudes and assumptions we create about who we are and how the world works.

It manifests also in the stories we tell ourselves and we then act according to those stories, so can you now see the importance of telling yourself the right story?

In a word, a mental inclination or disposition, or a frame of mind, your **mindset** is your collection of **thoughts** and **beliefs** that shape your thought habits, and your thought habits affect how you **think**, what you **feel**, and what you **do**. Your mind-set impacts how you make sense of the world, and how you make sense of you.

Never Underestimate the Power of BELIEF! A belief is a feeling that something is true or real even without firm or physical evidence

"Whether you think you can, or you think you can't, you're right."

Henry Ford

Think! Be very careful of your thoughts for they create your reality.

Your beliefs about yourself, your Vision, your world, affect your thoughts, your self-talk, (your inner voice that could often be more helpful), feelings, perceptions and results.

There are external forces ready to shake your self-belief. Opposition is bound to happen, it is human nature, sometimes we even sabotage our own success but reinforced self-belief and a vision that we are committed to will give us the strength to go on.

Mindset

Did you know that you can copy any 'state' that you have had in the past and feel the emotion related to it again whenever you want? That you can recall any powerful memory and feel the feelings associated with that memory?

How often do you use these to inspire or motivate yourself? Remind yourself of all the great things, the positive things you have done, overcome and succeeded at in the past. Think about your many achievements. Thoughts grow where focus goes!

These positive thoughts and memories together will lift a low mood and the more you practise it, the more skilled you become. Boost your confidence in this way and become enthusiastic about yourself again. You've experienced it before, therefore you can experience it again! Sometimes you just have to be your own best Cheerleader!

You could start on 21 days as Your Own Cheerleader and after this time it becomes an automatic daily habit!

You have navigated the choppy waters of life before and no doubt you will again, but you came through! When similar situations recur reflect on how you handled them previously. You are stronger than you think!

"You are stronger than you may ever know, until put to the greatest test".

Uncertainty and change are also unsettling and can cause us to over or even under-respond. You can just BE with the uncertainty of your feelings - you do not always need to react, especially if whatever is happening is not life threatening. Be kind to you. Allow yourself to breathe, take a calm approach.

Life is either an adventure or a perilous journey, depending on how you look at it. And without a doubt, if you expect the worse to happen it will, so be extra careful with your thoughts.

Deal only with what you can control. I have often said this about worrying: "If there's nothing you can do about the situation, then stop worrying because it is out of your hands anyway and worrying only makes you feel worse. If there IS something you can do about the situation then make the decision, and having made it, let it go!" That relieves pressure too.

Mindfulness

Live in the moment. This time is all we have now. However, live it fully from the knowing of your Inner Vision.

Breathing

It is not unusual, with the stresses of modern life, to get out of rhythm with our breathing, even to the extent of holding our breath without realising it. We need the oxygen we breathe for a heathy body and mind. Brainpower needs oxygen too! If you catch yourself holding your breath from time to time decide to either set yourself an alarm or create a trigger to remind you to spend a couple of minutes deep breathing.

You need to remain strong. When your perceptions are programmed, positive and directed towards your Vision you will attract what you need to succeed. To realise your Vision you must believe, think and act in the present as if it already exists.

Are your thoughts Positive or Negative?

Positive? Fantastic! Let's not change a thing!

Negative? Even if only just occasionally? Well, we are all human after all.

Remember that one positive thought early in the morning can change your whole day.

You tend to get what you expect. So why not expect something wonderful is about to happen!

So, let's make those negative episodes as short as possible, in fact eliminate them. That reminds me of a very appropriate song title. 'You've got to e-l-i-m-i-n-a-t-e the negative, a-c-c-e-n-t-u-a-t-e the positive, that's what gets results!'

There are many techniques to work on a negative mindset to move it towards positive. Why is this important? Because mindset mimics Beliefs and vice versa.

As sure as eggs are eggs, if you believe something strongly enough it WILL manifest, even if not exactly in the shape or form you imagined, but put simply imagining failure WILL lead to a failure of some sort and imagining success WILL bring success even if in slightly different form than you expected.

Negative thinking is based from Fear (False Evidence Appearing Real) and positive thinking is based from Courage.

Your thoughts and the actions that follow are your choice and no one else's. We always have choice. And we can change that choice at any given moment! It is vital to come into this programme believing in the right outcome from the start, knowing you have the benefit of those who have gone before that proves this works in wondrous ways. Be prepared to move out of your Comfort Zone, but in safe hands.

An Attitude of Gratitude?

Ever heard that saying? What it means is that when you add thoughts of Gratitude to the wonderful achievements in your life AND also to the not so wonderful, that perhaps taught you powerful lessons, then your vibrations shift up a notch in the right direction to attract more wonderful things into your life.

If you constantly need to remind yourself what you are grateful for, start a daily Gratitude Journal. Write it down. Include pictures, photos, drawings, snippets of material, Thank You cards or little notes people have sent you, whatever helps to colour those memories and enhance your feeling of Gratitude!

You'll be amazed in only a short time how this will positively affect your mindset.

Consider creating a gratitude mantra for your meditations or affirmations. Just a short phrase - perhaps as simple as "I am Grateful to be alive today!"

Try saying it to the person you see in your mirror each morning! A great habit to create.

The Gift That Keeps on Giving

Have you heard this one? What is the gift that keeps on giving, really? Its another attitude! Givers tend to find that they attract gifts! It seems to be a Universal law. To receive, you first need to give! Try it!

Other help

NLP

If maintaining a positive mindset in difficult times is a challenge, there is so much help available. NLP (Neuro Linguistic Programming techniques relate to thoughts, language, and patterns of behaviour learned through experience to specific outcomes).

Cognitive Behavioural Therapy

A range of therapies based on the theory that thoughts, feelings, what we do and how our body feels are all connected. How true!

We are complicated Creatures!

Posture, Expression, Visualising and other techniques to become more aware.

One powerful tip!

We all learn, take in information and create memories in different ways.

To create an environment for powerful memory and recollection incorporate movement, (stand, walk, dance), colour, audio, visuals and even odours into your exercise sessions, wherever possible. This creates a more active experience that engages all your senses, especially your emotions, and helps ground your learning deeper, into your cells, muscles and memory too!

Exercise 1:

To lift a mood, DO something different!

> ➤ Lift your gaze and look up instead of down. Practise looking up for a while, pausing and then looking down and hold for a while. How different do you feel after each?

> ➤ Try standing or sitting in different postures and become aware how each feels. Head up or down. Holding yourself upright or slumped, shoulders straight back or hunched. What differences do you notice?

> ➤ Power pose! Have a go at your Superman or Wonderwoman posture. Stand tall, head and shoulders back, Hands on hips. Legs slightly apart and facing forward. Put a smile on your face! How do you feel now?

> ➤ Have a go at pulling different facial expressions, for example, frown then smile and notice how different these make you feel

> ➤ Catch yourself in the mirror unintentionally and you may surprise yourself how different thoughts show up to others in your body language (although these can sometimes be misinterpreted!)

➢ Smile, sing along to a song, dance or tell a joke. Seeing someone else laugh has a positive ripple effect!

➢ Develop an Attitude of Gratitude daily with a log or diary

List three things you have learned from Exercise 1.

1.

_____

_____

_____

_____

2.

_____

_____

3.

_____

_____

_____

Exercise 2.

Snap Out of It! Do something Different - Pattern Breaking

If you want to get physical, then the "Stop That!" or "Snap Out of It!" Band is also useful for breaking negative patterns of behaviour by stopping, eliminating and replacing your own negative words and actions. It also helps when you are in a conversation that turns negative and you begin to join in! It is a 'trigger' that alerts your brain to action needed and the words are the instruction you are giving yourself.

Get yourself a rubber band, in a colour and thickness of your choice, that fits around your wrist with just a little room to spare.

Whenever you notice your Monkey (primitive) Brain bringing negative thoughts or criticism of yourself to mind, simply take hold of the band, pull it as far as you can away from your wrist and let it snap back while saying "Stop That - I am a capable resourceful person" or whatever other words you prefer to say after "Stop That", aloud or to yourself, depending on where you are at the time.

Make sure the band does create a little tingle. If for any reason you are unable to do this physically, work at visualising the band and imagining this action happening.

You need not alert anyone to what you are doing. I have used this neat little method while chairing a boardroom meeting - with my hands under the table and speaking to myself in my head!

Exercise 2.

Snap Out of It! Questions

1. What colour is your rubber band?

   _____

   _____

2. Is your rubber band imaginary or real? (Remember not to ping the real one too hard!)

   _____

   _____

   _____

3. How many times have you used the rubber band to Snap Out of It! this week?

   _____

   _____

   _____

4. What three things have you learned from using your rubber band this way?

1.

_____

_____

_____

_____

_____

2.

_____

_____

_____

3.

_____

_____

_____

_____

Exercise 3.

Do something Different - Create Your Security Dome

Imagine this! Your very own dome that shields you from external negative forces - looks, words, vibes, and auras.

Visualise this! In the mind's eye of your imagination construct a clear (transparent) glass dome. Imagine you are standing on a stage or in a room about to speak or have a conversation.

Feeling nervous? Concerned about what people will think or say or how they will respond with body language or facial expressions to your presence or what you are about to say?

Or in a general conversation that you expect to turn negative?

Now imagine this. The large glass dome, big enough to cover you and leave plenty of space for you to move about, begins to slowly come down from above over you. Hear your favourite song or music and notice the bright colour clothes you are wearing. Hear the music get louder as the dome comes lower, until it rests on the ground, encircling you 360°. The music stops there.

My favourite music for this is Thunderbirds Are Go! and it looks so funny when I demonstrate on video. I hope you'll get the chance to see it!

You can see and hear everyone around you, and they can see and hear you. You can breathe calmly and speak confidently.

Now there is something magical about this glass dome you have constructed.

As negative words, looks or vibes come towards you, they hit the dome, shrivel up, turn to dust, and fall away. They do not get in! Positive words, looks and vibes are allowed in!

Like a semi-permeable membrane, almost like your second skin, more gets out than gets in!

Which means that ALL the good that you want to share with the world, your words, looks, vibes and aura - do go out through the dome and benefit those around you and the world.

No one else can see this by the way! It's only in your imagination. And you can set a trigger to call this up whenever you want, by any gesture you choose, for example crossing your fingers, so that it is as natural as taking a deep breath - but you'll need to practise often until you can call it up at will.

Exercise 3.

Security Dome Questions

1. What music have you chosen to use for this technique?

_____

_____

2. How long did it take you to create this image?

_____

_____

3. When and where do you intend to use it?

_____

_____

4.What benefit do you feel you got from this exercise

_____

_____

Exercise 4.

To lift a mood, SAY something different! Change your words

When people ask "How are you?" or even when you are talking to yourself in your head, (as we all do!) what are you answering? "Oh, I'm OK" (as in I am not OK but I will say I am anyway) said with a shrug of the shoulders and a downward look. Or maybe you'll come out and say "I feel down" (or depressed overwhelmed, or whatever). Well whatever it was you said, you were exactly right.

Think about the words you use most to describe your feelings. First think of and write down any negatives you sometimes say and then think and write the opposite word which is a positive

1. Negatives

_____

_____

_____

_____

_____

2. Then say and write some 'positives'

_____

_____

_____

_____

_____

_____

3. What is the difference? How did this exercise make you feel?

_____

_____

_____

_____

_____

_____

In thinking the thoughts about your feelings and putting those into words, you ARE it! Remember the famous quote "I think, therefore I am" by René Descartes? We are back to thoughts become things because the moment you think it the brain sends a message to your body and into every cell, which then reacts and sets up a repeating Down Cycle. In time this becomes the habit.

So here is something else you can do to change this habit and bring in different words form new brain patterns of positive words to get you back into the Up Cycle

Mantras and Affirmations - Words

In its simplest form, create or learn a Mantra, write it down and display around your home and office where you will notice it every day. You could use the same one from your meditations for repetition and habit forming. Repeat it to yourself daily. Say it to yourself while meditating. It may be as simple as "I am positive and determined that my life is daily changing for better".

Another very similar form is to write one or more positive Affirmations. Focus on only one affirmation at a time until you know it well. Then you can move on to another. Your affirmation can be used as a note that you can place all around as a visual and almost subliminal reminder on your screensaver, calendar, mirror, fridge door, wherever you are likely to stop and look around your home or office during the day.

For both of these devices, make them eye catching in some way. It could be the colours you use, or a little cartoon to add, or something stuck on to the card or paper on which they are written. I give you permission to be your creative self!

Exercise 5.

Mantras and Affirmations Questions:

1. Which Key Positive Affirmation or Mantra have you chosen?

_____

_____

2. Where have you placed reminders, so far?

_____

_____

3. What have you done to make them eye catching?

_____

_____

4. What three benefits have you discovered so far from using Affirmations or Mantras?

1.

_____

_____

_____

2.

3.

Exercise 6.

What three key things have you learned from this chapter about consciously considering your mindset and how your thoughts come out in words and actions?

1.

_____

_____

_____

_____

2.

_____

_____

_____

_____

3.

_____

_____

_____

"To understand the immeasurable, the mind must be extraordinarily quiet, still"

Jiddu Krishnamurti

Chapter Five

STEP 1.i MASTER YOUR MINDFUL MEDITATION

No Yoga Pose Necessary. However, Relaxation Essential!

Why Meditate? What's In It For Me?

Meditation is essential prior to all the steps in the Destination Me™ programme in order for you to receive the best outcome.

Meditate - Oxford Concise English Dictionary

Focus one's mind for a time for spiritual purposes or relaxation

What is Meditation?

An encyclopedia could be written on the topic of Meditation alone and we don't have the time, space or need to go into all of this here. In a nutshell, meditation, specifically the guided meditation developed for the purposes of this book and the programme, over and above the description that follows, changes your state, to calm and relax you and open you up to creativity. As it does so it also raises your vibrational energy levels higher and connects you with your Heart, Mind, Body, Spirit to your Inner Vision Compass™ and the Universe.

Benefits of Meditation

The benefits of meditation are recorded as both mental and physical. In the context of Destination Me™ meditation changes your mental state to calmer and more open minded, receptive to the learning and experiences you are about to undergo. You are more relaxed and able to pull away from your left-brain logical thinking which usually dominates your daily thoughts and actions. You also become more in tune with your own intuition, connect with your more spiritual you and ready to open up and expand the creative space needed to go into the next step, Step 2, Clear Your Mind Clutter™

Why Meditate?

Apart from the opportunity to take time out and chill, perhaps to soak in the environment with Mindful Meditation, or listen to some relaxing music or inspirational guidance with obvious benefits, what's the most powerful aspect of Meditation for holistically improving your life? Meditation opens up fresh mind space for creativity, imagination and new ideas!

Why is meditation placed at the heart of the transformational Destination Me™ Programme, to practise before taking each of the Six Steps to Success? We know that Clients rave about their experience of the whole programme, including the guided meditations, which enable them to get "Out of their Head and into their Body, Heart and Spirit too"!

How Often should I meditate?

Meditation works best when formed into a daily habit. People ask me how frequently, how long and at what time they should meditate daily, and which is best.

Well, this is different for everyone. Some start, as I did with meditating for an hour each day, then after a period go to half an hour. Now I meditate for 9:56 minutes exactly, early each morning first thing before anything else.

This works for me and sets me up for the whole day. I listen to a music only soundtrack with calming sounds of the sea in the background.

Choices include these or guided meditations, where someone talks you through either the meditation itself or issues you want to address but I find the sound of someone else's words intrusive - it's a personal thing and the choice is yours. The important thing is to start and experiment until you find what help you get calmer, clearer, more able to have a purposeful and fulfilling day.

How difficult is it to meditate?

Here's a clue. Daydreamers are already part of the way there, except that daydreaming is mostly involuntary and is not planned and delivered at will, like meditation. Although you do need to be consistent in practice, one week of learning will prepare you enough to achieve the significant results Clients get with meditation during the programme.

We asked earlier, "What's in it for me?" Read on and find out....

Here's the science bit…...

Meditation was hailed as the "Cutting Edge Science of the New Millennium". It is a powerful process, when done correctly. Its use by millions and variety of techniques have grown exponentially since then. So, there must be something in it?

Scientists have now recognised for some years that our brains have neuroplasticity, which basically means that they are not permanently fixed. We can change and remould them. You can make fundamental changes to your brain and those changes can substantially change your experience of life AND the results you create.

For example, as you will see below, when you have sudden insights, 'Ah-Ha! Or Lightbulb Moments, (which Clients always have during their Destination Me™ Programme), you are making bursts of Theta waves in your brain.

When you create more Theta waves, you'll discover enhanced awareness, become more creative and generate solutions plus lots of new ideas.

Dr James McGaugh of the University of California at Irvine established the connection between memory and Theta. The more Theta waves, the better the memory. I believe this works in two ways: building your capacity to memorise but also improving your connectivity to the memories of your Inner Vital Vision, implanted at birth. When used prior to each of the Six #Steps to Success in the

Destination Me™ Programme this enhances your ability to embed your transformational experience subconsciously, in your memory and the very cells of your body. Your Vision then becomes "Vital" as it acquires I.M.P.A.C.T.

More about I.M.P.A.C.T. later…

The Purpose of Meditation is to "to Change your State" from the default or normal Beta rapidly reacting to the stresses and challenges arising every day, to one that is deeper, more relaxed and sleep-like, open and receptive, resourceful and creative.

States are created by different levels of Brainwaves. Brainwaves have different speeds and electrical frequencies (Imagine tuning to the right radio station). Each channel delivers something different for you.

When brainwaves slow down, something wonderful happens! The left and right brain hemispheres communicate much better, synchronicity and coherence occur for whole-brain functioning rather than sticking with our often-usual predominance of left-brain logic with its ego and inner critic!

As you move through the levels, Meta-Awareness arrives, increasing your mental powers! A new perspective, your view from the highest possible spot, (you will discover this through meditation AND during your Guided Meditation on your VIP Vital Vision™ Blueprint Session in Chapter 8) brings you insights, creativity, enhanced learning ability, improved memory AND……VISION!

Brainwaves operate at 5 different levels, speeds, frequencies

These are their patterns, states, speeds and impacts.

Gamma is the state of Compassion. These are the fastest brainwaves and when embedded within Theta waves they deliver the Ultimate Loving Kindness State.

Delta is the state of Dreamless Sleep. These are the slowest brainwaves that deliver a feeling of Oneness. Delta waves release beneficial brain chemicals that slow ageing, bring leadership qualities, persuasion abilities and achievement. They are attributed to Kundalini Awakening.

Theta is the state of Dreaming sleep. Slower brainwaves, left-right brain connection, integrative experiences, creativity and bypasses self-sabotage to deliver Ah-ha moments and visionary experiences.

Alpha state brings relaxed readiness with slower brainwaves that open up creativity and enable super-learning. A state just between sleeping and awaking.

Finally, Beta, the normal waking state. Faster brainwaves, everyday default mode, complete consciousness.

The art of Meditation takes practice. It may seem difficult at first but improves over time when practised consistently with small daily actions.

The length of time you meditate is your choice. If 'time' is an issue then rising that little bit earlier to meditate will set you up for a more positive, energised, focused and creative day.

In addition to daily starting your day with a meditation routine, there are specific instances where being able to raise your State with meditation at will is a valuable tool to open up your creativity and enhance your cognition and learning. This is the primary reason for introducing you to meditation practice right at the start of your Destination Me™ journey and lies at the heart of the programme.

You can choose from a wide variety of types of meditation or create your own once you are familiar with the process.

NOW Here's the REALLY GREAT NEWS!

You do NOT have to spend years practising meditation before you are able to change your life and your world!

The specific way in which we have created the Destination Me™ Intensive Programme delivers transformational change at any point in the journey and especially during your Vital Vision™ Blueprint session.

Over 20 years of research, learning, experience, creation, delivery, testing, measuring results, adapting and developing have been built into this programme, delivering amazing results in much less than 30 Days and it will work for you too!

So How do I meditate?

Follow your Environment Checklist to prepare for meditation.

Ensure that you have a reasonably comfortable chair, comfortable, casual clothes, a device to play your music on. You can meditate with or without music. Provided you find the method that works for relaxing you into a calm, peaceful state, it is your choice. In this programme music is essential, however.

Be seated, start the music, sit comfortably with your feet flat on the ground and relax. Close your eyes and set up your breathing rhythm.

Meditating outdoors, in a garden or in nature, where there is fresh air and provided it is quiet, apart from perhaps the sounds of birdsong or running water which are calming sounds, is especially good for you.

B-r-e-e-e-a-t-h-e

Breathe in through your nose, deeply, into your belly and hold the breath to the count of three, then breathe out deeply and hold your breath to the count of three. Repeat this five, or six times and then relax into a slow breathing rhythm as you listen to the soundtrack.

You can choose a timed soundtrack or use a timer to alert you when you have meditated for your chosen length of time. Meditating is very personal and different for everyone, so practise until you get it right for you. You should notice a feeling of calm, clarity and focus when you get it right for you, and time passes without you realizing it.

When you are very experienced, you will be able to put yourself into state to create those same feelings anytime during the day, without necessarily listening to music but by your mind and body remembering.

Meditation is essential to creating the right state to engage fully with every exercise throughout the programme described in this book.

If you have meditated before and are well versed in the practice, ensure that you do so before every exercise in this book.

However if you have never meditated, or perhaps have attempted to meditate before and did not feel it was working for you, I highly recommend taking the Seven Day Learn to Meditate course offered at the time of writing, by Insight Timer and other sites include

'Headspace' and 'Online Meditation'.

Meditation need not become time consuming and No, you do not have to assume a yoga or any other specific position!

I sit comfortably early in the morning and meditate for exactly nine minutes and fifty-six seconds. This clears my head when I focus on doing so and sets me up well for a great day every day!

There are at least two ways to use meditations.

> To open up creative space and get clarity, play calming music, focus on your breath and breathing, repeat a Mantra. Each time you notice thoughts intruding, accept them, say thank you, not needed right now, let them go and focus back on your breathing and repeating your Mantra.

> To use meditation to generate new ideas, set that intention and don't use your Mantra; listen to the music and let thoughts wander and flow then jot them down for further exploration or action.

Meditations Exercise 1.

1. Which meditation platform have you chosen? Clue: Insight Timer. Headspace. Other.

_____

_____

2. Which types of meditation have you explored?
Clue: Music Only. Guided. Both

_____

_____

3. Does your provider enable analytics or rewards so you can see your progress?

_____

_____

4. What is your new daily meditation routine?

_____

_____

Meditations Exercise 2

List 3 benefits you feel you have received from meditating.

1.

_____

_____

_____

2.

_____

_____

3.

_____

_____

_____

4. How often will you continue to meditate regularly?

_____

_____

_____

You Cannot Fill a Cup That is Already Full

Lao Tzu

CONGRATULATIONS!
PREPARE TO CREATE HEAD SPACE

Chapter Six

STEP 2 CLEAR YOUR MIND CLUTTER

Time to clear out the internal filing cabinets of your mind and get rid of your mental baggage.

If you can answer Yes to any of the following questions, then you are most definitely READY for the start of your journey, so let's do something about it!

Are you experiencing or feeling?-

Trapped by crisis	☐
Being called or needing to change	☐
Unclear or confused about the future	☐
'Stuck' or 'Blocked'	☐
In Overwhelm	☐
Too many or not enough choices	☐
Too many or not enough directions	☐
Not sure what to do next or first	☐
Confidence issues	☐
Limiting Beliefs holding you back	☐
Uncertainty about your future	☐
Stuck in your Comfort Zone and you know it	☐

Unclear on your Vision for the Life/Business you REALLY Want	☐
At a crossroads and caught in the middle	☐
In a period of Change	☐
Have experienced a Significant Emotional Event	☐
Anything else that is stopping you Living the Life You Love	☐

Where does this Clear Your Mind Clutter™ come from?

Well, there's a story behind it……

During an horrific road traffic accident, a football coach travelling at 60 miles per hour ploughed into the back of the car taking me, my daughter and her friend out one sunny day.

I was the back-seat passenger in the days before seatbelts. We were shunted into a sandwich filling between the coach and a stationary car in front of us, waiting to turn right.

Just before the impact (remember that word) I felt a touch on my left shoulder (no, I cannot explain it - I was alone in the back seat of the car with no one beside or behind me!). This prompted me to turn and look behind and see the speeding bus bearing down on us.

I screamed loudly "Get down, it's not going to stop". In a flash I glimpsed my daughter's surprise and fear in the rear-view mirror as I ducked into the emergency position I had learnt when flying.

Hardly had chance to get the words out, but they probably saved all of our lives, when the impact hit. As you can imagine, being faced with death was the most traumatic experience of my life.

It's true - there is a tunnel and a bright light. Everything seemed to happen in slow motion for a split second after the impact. Believing I was about to die, I prayed as I have never prayed. Quickly, over and over, "Please God take me not her (my daughter), take me not her".

As I moved toward the light, my life flashed rapidly before my eyes. Suddenly, I realised something had been missing. Instantly my belief shifted, and I found myself repeating "No, I'm not ready to go. I haven't fulfilled my purpose - I'll change, I will change!"

Pungent smoke invaded my nostrils. Seeing the car bonnet raised, I panicked, fearing fire or explosion. Trying to get out, I was pinned at head and neck by the parcel shelf that had shot forward on impact. I passed out and awoke in hospital.

An examination revealed a head injury, concussion, whiplash, knee injury, plus extensive bruising and swelling. Added to this I was in considerable pain.

Released the same day, we thought that was the end of it. In reality, it was the start of a two-year long nightmare. I experienced physical pain, constant nightmares and day-mares; flash backs, rerunning the video in my mind uninvited - seeing the bus approaching; my daughter's expression; hearing the noise, smelling the smells and feeling the physical **impact** over and over.

Remember that word impact, it has a huge bearing on every one of us and the intensity of our experiences and memories and how they affect us. Experiencing impact was to become key to how the Destination Me™ 6 Step programme shared in this book was developed.

Becoming unable to drive myself (mental images and mindset)

and detesting the experience, I turned into a nightmare passenger (I'm told!). I couldn't focus, concentrate, or think about anything but this accident.

Short-term memory loss followed, along with a condition similar to Dyslexia. I misspelt words and my sentences didn't make sense.

When a psychiatrist asked me to describe what was happening, I said it was as if someone had clambered into my head and ransacked all the filing cabinets.

There was chaos! Papers (thoughts and memories) everywhere and in no order whatsoever. I couldn't find anything (thoughts and memories) I needed, when I needed it!

Diagnosed with Post-Traumatic Stress Disorder (PTSD), the next two years were filled with tests, counselling, psychotherapy, physiotherapy, drugs, more drug, and knock-on effects set in.

Why the physio? Because of the constant pain I was experiencing, I had to be re-examined a month or so after being examined in accident and emergency, and it was only then discovered that the top three vertebrae of my spine had been fractured and crushed! It took some years to recover from these injuries.

Unable to work, I was forced to resign my Directorship of a leading Management Training Development Company. My own successful Management Consultancy went rapidly downhill.

Experiencing loss of income, a restricted budget, car and mortgage arrears, and for the first time; debt, deep depression set in. Until then, I'd always been positive minded and driven.

Now, I was like a little girl lost! Life was a major struggle. I felt so worthless, in despair, desperately sad and unhappy at times that I even contemplated suicide.

I just couldn't see my future or a way out of this. I was at rock bottom 101.

Why am I telling you this? Because I hope you'll realise that whatever issues you face or however low you have fallen, you can rise again. When you're at rock bottom, the only way is up!

Then something strange happened! My family bought me the most unexpected gift for my birthday that year. And I am forever grateful. It's one of those instances I describe as 'Opportunities Disguised as Challenges'.

At breakfast, on my birthday, I was handed a large white envelope. Wondering what this was, I opened it carefully and must have looked an absolute picture as my eyes widened in disbelief. Inside was a card announcing A One Day Driving Experience in a Formula First Car at the Racetrack! Imagine my initial horror! Dreading even being a passenger in a car, I'm being faced with driving one.

Not just any car, by the way, but a racing car. My first instinct was to say "Thank you very much but you know I can't do this" but looking at my son's face, as he said "You CAN do this mum", what could I do? I knew then I had no choice, I had to do this. For my family, for him and for me.

After much protesting I had finally said "Yes", while still thinking to myself, I can still call it off if I get there and don't like it.

Off we went to the racetrack. Once there I was led into a classroom where I sat through the instructor's briefing, all the while thinking, "This is so complicated, I'll never get the hang of it"! Remember, my memory was completely out of kilter at that time and things that would normally be done by habit, I really had to concentrate to make sense of. My subconscious was not very cooperative!

Something the instructor said about not letting the revs (engine revolutions) drop or the engine would cut out stuck with me. After the initial terror, when the crew had padded behind me with cushions so my feet could reach the pedals, adjusted my helmet and goggles, we were go!

The words "Don't let the revs drop" kept going round in my head and after a shaky start I put my foot down on the accelerator and don't think I ever lifted it until I finally came to stop!

Although this was a proper sized racetrack, my family standing at the side of the track observing seemed to whizz by me every couple of minutes and nervous as I was, I also began to feel excited and exhilarated…

Later, visibly shaking as I went into the debriefing, I discovered that in my attempt to keep the revs up I had been taking the bends at sixty miles an hour! Which also explained why I had been lapping everyone. I now felt more alive than I had for the past two years! I knew then that I was most definitely on the way back!

Such experiences are miracles and eventually are recognized as gifts. For me, it became the foundation of the purpose I had prayed about in the accident. Reconnecting with my self-belief, I took this as a sign.

Instead of going to counselling the next day, for the first day of many, I went to the library. Study became my new habit. Books taught me so much. I studied healing; trauma; psychology; NLP; Mind, Body and Spirit; the brain, neurology, Positive Thinking plus inspiration from entrepreneurs and, leaders.

I worked through all the exercises and mastered the techniques, especially CBT and NLP. I lost myself in books, devouring meditation, belief, confidence, inspiration and, studying people who had turned their lives around.

What they all had in common was strong belief and with that clarity, focus and direction and I was now rebuilding my own, along with new understanding, empathy and uncovering my unique gifts. I was finding my way back from a very dark place to my true self and my why and really appreciating and having gratitude for the joy of life itself.

My purpose was clear. I'd been given a second chance to create a legacy, to leave the world a better, more wonderful place. By sharing the gifts arising from my experiences I could help as many people as possible to break through blocks, barriers and challenges.

Now I could help business owners and entrepreneurs like you to tune into their own power and to create the wonderful life, business, career, world, whatever they really want.

I learned from my own IMPACTful experiences how to create the process to turn into the Vision, Values and Beliefs aligning work, silencing your Inner Critic and preventing external or self-sabotage to achieve exceptional results quickly.

I learned how to step outside of my experience and observe it. I learned how to reshape and reframe my memories.

I learned that all we need is still inside of us and we need to trust and follow our own intuition.

And I learned that in order to create calm out of chaos we need to Clear the Mind Clutter.

The clearing methods I employ were taught me by a Shaman who successfully took me through this process to heal and clear my mind, body and spirit and I share one of these methods with you here.

Life and time are too precious to spend stuck. The way to get unstuck is to change, and change takes courage. Knowing you are making the right choices and going in the right direction speeds you towards your purpose, goals and dreams, building your confidence and belief in the process.

When this comes from your Heart, Mind, Body and Spirit you can trust it completely. My life is unrecognisable now!

After experiencing my own successes I began to share what I knew with others and this led to their successes, which felt wonderful because helping people to overcome their challenges and enjoy their lives is my Purpose and Passion and it is why I want to help you too.

The thing is this - Everything IS Possible - but first you must be absolutely clear on what you want and then there are certain steps you need to take to get it. And I have the complete system for you! IF that's what you want. BUT you have to be READY - to have had enough of living the way you are and want it to be so much better.

TODAY, in this chapter, in my desire to help you move forward happily to your greater abundance, I am sharing with you Step 2 'Clear Your Mind Clutter'™. This step can be done with a facilitator, but within this little book I show you the DIY option - all you need to know for how to go through this process for yourself.

As you will read, it is essential to be relaxed and in a calm environment without distractions when you go for Clear Your Mind

Clutter™. This powerful process needs a meditation beforehand. If you already have your own meditation resources, then use them.

Before you begin, check your Environment List in the Appendices and prepare the space you will be working in. Have a pen and notepaper or sticky notes pad to hand.

After you have used your meditation to relax, then play your favourite relaxing soundtrack (without lyrics is essential) to go through the clearing activity which you will find below with the explanation of why you need to clear the mind clutter before attempting to open up your creative process to start anything new that's vitally important to you - and what could be more important than finally getting to live life the way you REALLY want?

This is the MOST IMPORTANT WORK you can do TODAY!

Why do you need to 'Clear Your Mind Clutter™' before you set out on the best journey of your life - to Destination Me™?

Because you can't fill a cup that is already full! Read on...

The Overflowing Cup

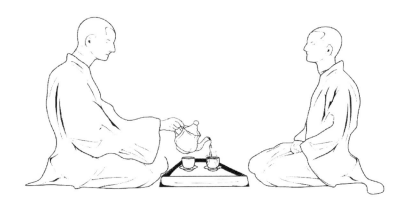

A master was trying to explain something to a student who already had knowledge and experience aplenty to draw upon. But each time the master tried to explain something new to the student he would hold it up against his own notions of the way the world is and how it ought be, and was unable to see the lessons the master was trying to teach him.

Finally, the master poured a full serving of tea into his own cup, and into the cup of the student. He told the student he wanted to give to him some of the tea from his own cup and began pouring that tea into the student's cup, but since the student's cup was already full, all of the master's tea spilled out over the cup onto the surface below.

The student said, "Master, you can't pour anything into my cup until I empty it to make room for what you are trying to give me.", and the master replied "Yes I know."

"And I can't give you any new thoughts or ideas or perspectives on life's lessons until you clear out some thoughts that are already teeming in your mind to make room for what I have to teach you."

Then the master paused for one brief moment. Meeting the student's eyes with his own knowing look, gently, calmly but sternly he then said:

"*If you truly seek understanding, then first, empty your cup!*" At this point, the student understood....

Do you get this? Before we can create the new, we need some space.

TIME to 'Clear Your Mind Clutter'-Let's Go to It AND Let it Go!

The most important aspect of this step is that you take your time! Do not rush!

Even if you think or feel that you have no baggage to clear - sit with the exercise as described for at least half an hour to see what comes up. Most people will have issues, frustrations, decisions unmade, important or not, whether recent or from the past, self-induced or caused by people or events around them. Even trivial issues are baggage if not settled.

Anything that you find thoughts about interrupting your day or coming back to you inconveniently is a message that requires attention. When you block it, this becomes unfinished business and has nowhere to go but round and round in your head, taking up space and bound to come up again and again!

Clearing of **'baggage'** is essential in order to open up mind space in order to allow the new in to stimulate new ideas, generate solutions, maximise your creative potential, benefit and opportunities. And remember, you can use this technique time and time again and you will become more proficient is quickly dealing with situations that before would have had you 'stuck'.

This is the time to release those thoughts, negative feelings, uncertainty, emotions especially 'unfinished business' and baggage, all of which have held you back from living the life and business you REALLY want.

Step 2 - Part One - Pre-Clearing Preparation

Begin with preparing yourself for Clearing. If you have a favourite meditation, either guided or simply a music track you love, use this to relax you, to take you to a place of peace and serenity before you begin the Clearing.

Light your scented candle then start the music or guided meditation you will use <u>before</u> the Clearing. Be seated with your feet (preferably bare to make the better connection with the earth below you) placed flat on the ground. Sit comfortably with your hands in your lap, close your eyes and concentrate on your deep breathing.

Take deep breaths through your nose, one, two, three, and hold. Deep breaths out through your mouth, one, two, three and hold. Repeat five or six times while listening to the music until you feel calm, relaxed and settle into a comfortable slow breathing routine. You will know when you are ready to move on to the Clearing process.

Before you begin, another reminder. Recognise that doing this exercise requires you to take some time, do not rush it.

Step 2 - Part Two - The Clearing

From this point, play music only - no voice or lyrics - so that you can concentrate. You need to focus on the thoughts and feelings that come in. Do not force, just remain calm and relax to the music.

Be honest with yourself. Ask the right question to begin, **"What are the issues that are still troubling me that no longer serve me and that I now choose to let go?"**

Allow yourself to open up to your thoughts and feelings with the intention to clear that which no longer serves you. Bring up into your consciousness what it is that has been troubling you, blocking you, holding you back, creating fear, negative emotions, stress, frustration.

Include unmade decisions that you have been pondering, no matter how insignificant or even major it may seem. Just let the thoughts come in and notice the context, especially anything that is genuinely clutter only that you can clear straight away.

As each thought comes in give it your attention. Is the matter unresolved? If so, ask what you can do to resolve it. If it cannot be resolved, you have a choice. Will it serve you to let go?

If you should feel there is some unfinished business that still needs action to clear then jot a note on a sticky note or pad for what you need to do to resolve it and make this a priority to act upon in the next two days, for your own satisfaction - and for the good of all concerned. Pop the note on an Action pile to be dealt with later.

Is it resolved already? Perhaps. Why is it coming back? Some element overlooked. Sit with it and ask. You now have the choice. Each time you are prepared to let something go, imagine you see yourself writing the thought on a sticky note or slip of paper. Place each note on a separate Disposal pile and keep going.

When no further thoughts are coming in, or you feel that you have spent enough time for now, see yourself taking the pieces of paper from the Disposal pile and placing them in a paper bag or sack. Your choice!

Now see yourself take the paper bag or sack to a crackling blazing bonfire that comes into your view. Throw the paper bag or sack, contents and all, onto the bonfire and marvel as all this baggage goes up into beautiful colourful flames rising and flickering and throwing sparks like stars high into the night sky, and notice that you now do not even recall what the baggage was.

It's as if they never were and you are released from holding on to those cares any longer to make way for new exciting thoughts and ideas to come in as you move forward on your journey

If you should feel that there is some unfinished business that still needs action to clear it, then note what you need to do to resolve it. For your own satisfaction, and for the good of all others concerned, make this a priority to act upon in the next two days.

As you come back to your fully awakened state, open your eyes and observe your surroundings, remain conscious of any issues on your Action pile and schedule time to deal with these as a matter of urgency to set you free.

Now on your journey to Destination Me™ you leave behind that which does not serve you.

Since a Cluttered Environment reflects in a Cluttered Mind, this would be the right time to think about clearing your physical environment too, of those items taking up space around you that you know you no longer need.

What you may take for granted so much that you no longer notice it may be something that someone else may have a real need for. Remember that 'giving' as well as 'clearing' both have ways of lifting the spirits….as well as creating space to think, move and be!

You are progressing wonderfully! Congratulations for getting this far! Now you need to **Keep going!**

Clear Your Mind Clutter™ Exercise Questions:

1. Why do you think it is important to Clear Your Mind Clutter?

_____

_____

2. For how long did you work on the actual Clearing process?

_____

_____

3. For how long did you meditate immediately prior to doing the Clearing?

_____

_____

4. What challenges did you face in visualising the Clearing of your baggage?

_____

_____

_____

5. Do you consider that you have completed this exercise fully or will you need to revisit it?

_____

_____

6. What three things have you learned from going through Clear Your Mind Clutter™

1.

_____

_____

_____

2.

_____

_____

_____

3.

_____

_____

_____

7. What three benefits have you discovered so far from using Clear Your Mind Clutter™?

1.

2.

3.

8. In your own words say what you think and feel about your experience of Clear Your Mind Clutter™

You're Always Just A Hair's Breadth From

Success,

Opportunities Disguised As Challenges,

Keep Going To Live The Life Of Your Dreams!

Chapter Seven

STEP 3 VITALISE YOUR VALUES

Congruence is Key!

"Success is achieved when your Vision aligns with your Values, so being clear on your Values is Vital".

First, some quick reminders. Take your time! Do not rush! Deep thinking required. Check your Environment List in the Appendices. Have pen and paper to hand. Remember to meditate before doing the exercise.

When you go through the next chapter, to work on creating your Vital Vision™ Blueprint for the life you love, indeed any time you are thinking and planning for your life and your future, always be very clear on your values.

Making that check in with yourself can prevent many sometimes expensive detours from your path in terms of either time, money, or health for unsuccessful situations from relationships to business and work, in fact every aspect of your life.

Knowing your values, which are intrinsic to your intuition, is the key to harmony in your life and is essential to how you live it, and who with, at work, rest and play.

Knowing your values and working with them will get you

through good times and bad times, chaos, crisis and celebrating success.

However ambitious and grand an entrepreneur's Vision, their Values must be fully aligned to it.

So that we have a mutual understanding, and because this message is so important to success in every endeavour, let's take a quick look at what the Oxford Concise English Dictionary says about Vitalise and Values.

Vitalise: give strength and energy to something

Values: Principles and standards of behaviour, worth, importance, beneficial

Because your Values ARE so fundamental to success, I wanted to explain this in the simplest terms.

Whenever you get that churning stomach and your gut feeling stops you from going ahead on any decision or with something you or others planned, your core values are being tested.

You are being nudged to check in with yourself and trust, even if the answer seems logically Yes. Trust that you will receive the right answer through your intuition, even if this is No!

Whenever you can, sleep on that decision and you will have the right answer in the next day.

What are Values? However you describe them, Values are the inherent Code by which we live. What we deeply believe in at a subconscious as well as conscious level

- First, think about and list all your Values

- Then, order your Values into a hierarchy of Core Values

- Finally, do some reflection, think thoroughly about these Values, and consider any areas which are incongruent with the life you are living now.

- Remember that some Values can change in priority, come to the fore or draw back, as we live and our lives change. Rarely do our core Values completely change although they can be affected by traumatic incidents

Check your Values with your Vision for your life and business.

Do they align, match, correlate?

Yes? Then you are Setting Yourself Up For Success

No? Then think carefully before you continue

Why is it vital to have your Values aligned with your ambitious Vision?

The two critical reasons fundamental to success are this: -

1. Creating a Vision that conflicts with your Values, you are liable to self-sabotage your plans - therefore we check for potential conflicts within the process and create strategies to deal with any that arise

2. Working with people to achieve your Vision, but whose Values disagree with your own is setting yourself for conflict, disagreements, sabotage, and possible failure.

You will be able to think of many examples where these conflicts arise in your own life and circumstances.

Example 1:

You are passionately committed to protecting resources and the natural environment and love nature.

How will you succeed in selling the idea of a product or service that requires excessive packaging, potential waste or extensive tree felling out of context.

What effect does that have on you? Reflect and think of your own real-life examples where you have worked so hard and tried but failed to succeed in situations or endeavours.

Example 2:

Honesty and truth are your Core Values.

What if your work brings you into contact or requires co-operation with people you discover struggle with telling the truth or blatantly lie.

What effect does that have on you? Reflect and think of your own real-life examples where you have worked so hard and tried but failed to succeed in relationship situations.

Think about your own circumstances and where you have struggled to achieve in some area, look to identify either of the areas of conflict above you will begin to see why some plans are already doomed at the outset, so need rethinking, and why some relationships will never work - and you may need to decide whether to continue to compromise your values, or to walk away and in the future be aware so that you find the situations and relationships that work better for you.

Here's your Values Prompt!

Purpose	Security
Passion	Adventure
Truth	Strength
Honesty	Success
Integrity	Contribution
Love	Authenticity
Fidelity	Family
Motivation	Courage
Freedom	Sustainability
Happiness	Commitment
Inspiration	Legacy
Comfort	Giving

There are many more Values that we have not mentioned here. If you need more prompts, a quick Google will bring you more to consider.

However, what is important is to recognise the ones that are vital for you. There they are, hiding in your subconscious! Let's bring your values into your consciousness now.

Values: Be aware. Find the Perfect Values Match for you. What are yours? Take some time out to list your strongest Values now, and ensure they fit with your Vision. Enlighten yourself!

Vitalise Your Values:

Exercise 1.

Part 1:

First, practise a brief meditation to clear your thoughts and to get in tune with your intuition before going through this exercise

Then, Find 5 coloured pens and some paper, or use the exercise sheet on the next page.

Take your time.

Sit and write a list of your Values.

If you need a prompt revisit the value words list above

Think also in terms of what gives your life joy, happiness, satisfaction, contentment, what happens when you are in flow.

List as many values words to make the list as long - or short as you wish but - take your time - and visualise your values in action and interaction rather than just quickly jot down a list of words

Exercise 1.

Part 2:

When you feel you have finished the list of your values, take your first colored pen and create a Core Value Category by circling around the ones that have a connection - for example around Family and giving them that name

Take the second colored pen and circle around another group of values that are related to a topic or theme - for example around Business as a Core Value category name.

Take the third colored pen and circle around another group of values related to another topic or theme as a Core Value category name.

And do the same with the remaining colored pens.

With any values words left over, give them categories anyway. They are still your values and what is important is that you have now become more aware and reacquainted yourself with them.

Exercise 1.

Part 3:

Now that you have identified your 5 Core Values from the coloured bubbles of values words, list them. There is no particular order because when are put to the ultimate test, each of these is equally important.

Now think about your Core Values. These demonstrate who you are and what is important to you. To live life in flow and harmony, do not ever compromise on them no matter how attractive the proposition may be

How can you test your Core Values are real? Well, we have already referred to this earlier in the chapter.

Think back to a heated discussion or argument you have had with someone. What was it about? At the root of that argument or communication you'll find that one or more of your values was being dismissed or challenged and you were defending it!

Make life easier on yourself. Check in from time to time that life revolves around your Core Values.

Congratulations! Considering your Core Values before embarking on major change, indeed before making every major decision, is time well spent! Now for those exercises.

Exercise 1

Part 4:

Some values can shift and flow over time due to life experiences and events but essentially align with our heart, and they show themselves in our thoughts, words and actions.

When you are in Flow you can know you are truly aligned with your values. Think about your days. What do you love? What lights up your life? Fill the Exercise 4 page with all the things that give you JOY!

Exercise 2.

Part 1: LIST your Values below as they occur to you....

Exercise 2.

Part 2: LIST Your 5 key Core Values from the colored Values Categories bubbles in Exercise Part 3

1.

_____

_____

_____

2.

_____

_____

3.

_____

_____

_____

4.

_____

_____

_____

5.

_____

_____

Exercise 2.

Part 3:

Now think about instances in your life where it IS clear there is an obvious conflict with your Values.

Jot down just one key instance where conflict with your Values is recurring and where there is the possibility to take action to prevent this conflicting further and where by doing so you will not harm anyone but will make your life easier, more joyful and fulfilling.

Having thought about this you can decide what your options are. It is purely your choice whether or not you go ahead and change something - or not.

Exercise 4.

List the things and activities you Value, that light up your life and give you joy:

_____

_____

_____

_____

_____

_____

_____

_____

_____

_____

_____

_____

Exercise 5.

What three things have you learned from this chapter?

1.

2.

3.

'When you have a powerful, exciting and crystal-clear Vision for how you can create your life and your world, everything changes! And THAT'S when the Magic! Happens

Chapter Eight

STEP 4 VEST YOUR VITAL VISION BLUEPRINT

If You Can Imagine It, You Can Create It,
If You Can Dream It, You Can Become It!

Wm Arthur Ward

Never allow yourself to think that your vision is too big to handle. Discover your Why and you will find the Way. Your wonderful Imagination, your Trust and Belief, are crucial to the success of this step.

THIS IS YOUR MOST IMPORTANT WORK YOU CAN DO TODAY! ARE YOU READY?

This chapter is the powerful core of the programme. You are about to embark on an experience!

Your greatest opportunity for change in your present and for drawing this in through your Vital Vision™ Blueprint, the bright future of potential that you desire and recognize that begins today!

Consider your blueprint as your map for your life and your world that pictures both your destination and your journey!

Vision

Your Inner Vision knows itself. It consists of something far more powerful than anything you can create using cut images from a magazine and pasting them onto a Vision Board. You can do that later, if you want to 'pretty up' your Vision.

First though it is essential you work through the process in this chapter which has been specifically designed to ensure you go through the **I.M.P.A.C.T.F.U.L.** process and **EXPERIENCE** your Inner Vision and birth it into the world.

I - Imagination to Dream, Design, Create the life you REALLY want

M - Magic Insights! With Manifestation

P - Powered! Silenced Inner Critic, Subconscious SuccessSATNAV™

A - Attraction! The Secret, Law of Attraction and Cosmic Ordering

C - Creation! And Connection!

T - Transformation! With Traction. Leverage that Accelerates!

F - Flow

U - Universe Unlimited

L - Living Legacy!

Knowing, experiencing, seeing, feeling, and believing with clarity, focus and direction, what you want, what you are ready to receive and what you will receive.

This taps into your feelings and emotions, and so is formed in a very special way that works at your subconscious level.

Recognise that everything in the World and the Universe are

connected. You are connected too. Your life and your business are connected too, as are your family, friends, acquaintances, associates, clients, colleagues and so on. The world and the universe are systems and systems of systems.

Probably you have heard the quote about the Butterfly Effect. The things that change the world, according to **Chaos theory**, are the tiny things. A **butterfly flaps its wings** in the Amazonian jungle, and subsequently a storm ravages half of Europe.

Simply put, everything you do affects something else. For example, actions in your business affect your personal or family life in some way and personal or family related actions also affect your business life.

This emphasizes the need for the visioning process to be holistic, in effect encompass ALL of you, the individual you and the person you are in business. Even though you may separate out these elements later, for the visioning you are permitting and allowing ALL of your world to show up.

Where and how this real transformation takes place is usually achieved with a powerful specific spoken guided meditation that raises and transfers energetic vibration in real time and this is a core component included in the programme. Now, you are asked to place yourself into that powerful guided meditation, detailed below, giving your imagination full rein and visualizing in your head before going to work on externalizing your Inner Vision into your blueprint.

Have every confidence that in working through this book and completing all the exercises to bring you to this point you are capable, provided you feel ready! Only do this exercise on a day when you feel fully prepared.

You have worked on improving your meditation ability and your mindset, considered your thoughts and beliefs and what results from them, and cleared your mind clutter to open up creative space in readiness for this next step where you have the power to design the life you really want, now and in your future.

Have faith! You will do it! You are perfectly able and have all you need within you! Persevere with this vital session.

Now is the perfect time (always!) to create your Vital Vision™ Blueprint for your life and everything in it. It will inspire you and it will inspire others who have the will and resources to help you make it happen.

Until you export your vision into the outside world and TAKE RIGHT ACTION, it will remain a dream. Take your time and enjoy this exercise!

Before continuing check your Environment List and gather your materials

Choose the size of paper you want to work with and set your coloured pens out ready.

Prepare to light your scented candle and start your music playing. Classical music, no words, works best for this session.

Read the Rules. You may want to set your video recorder too!

Reviewing the recording afterwards, you may be surprised at what you see!

Get ready for The MOST IMPORTANT WORK YOU CAN DO TODAY!

Preparation:-

- Prepare yourself for an adventure. What is more exciting than time to imagine and design your own future?

- **I give you permission to create the future you really want. You need to give yourself permission too**

- Accept no limitations, we are in the realm of possibility. In fact 'Everything is Possible' provided that you see it clearly enough, believe it deeply enough and remind yourself often enough

A facilitated Visioning process, with an expert facilitator in this method, will add considerable value and an extra dimension as well as guiding you, keeping you on track, motivating you and seeing this through to the finished result with you. You can get this further help through the online programme Destination Me™

RULES:

Emphatically NO TALKING while you create your Blueprint, you want to quieten your Inner Critic. Only when you feel your Blueprint is complete is the time to SPEAK it out, record it and write down the elements of the Blueprint in the order you created them ready to Stormproof Your Success Strategies™ and Manifest Your Magnificent Masterplan™ all that you need to step out on your new journey into your new life. So QUIET PLEASE! until your vision is out into the world! Then you can SHOUT!

If unwanted negative thoughts drift in while you are doing this, accept they are trying to serve, say you are OK, and let them drift away again. Concentrate only on the music, and what comes in to serve your drawing.

Weave everything you want into your Vital Vision™ Blueprint, even if it may seem outrageous right now. Here are your Rules

- No speaking, humming, singing

- **Listen! To music (no lyrics) as you work**

- **Do not sit down.** Walk around the table as you create your blueprint. **This is also the process of embedding into your subconscious**

- **Use only one colour for the first 10 minutes**, then choose another for the next 10 minutes, then you are free to use all colours for the rest of this session. The colours you choose provide an expert facilitator with more clues about you that they will feed back or you can explore the meanings of colours

- **No use of written words, numbers, characters, symbols, logos on your Blueprint.** OK so that is difficult but use your imagination! **This is also the process of embedding into your subconscious**

- You're not recreating a work of art so if stick people is your thing, that's absolutely OK, so long as you include some image, whatever that may be, to represent each element that you see in your mind's eye of what you want, that is all that matters

- **When you think that you have really finished, ask yourself this. If this were absolutely my last and only chance to create the future I really want, what is still missing? Then give yourself 5 more minutes. It is surprising how many people suddenly have that creative rush toward the end.**

Note that this process can take half a day or longer. Allow adequate time to meditate and relax (state is important) to create your Blueprint, have a final check that all you want is in your Vital Vision™ and embedded.

So here we go…

Meditate twice for this chapter. First your usual calm down and relax daily meditation about one hour before working through this guided meditation which lasts as long as you want it to, the purpose being to imagine and visualize your Vital Vision™ and all that is in it before you begin to commit to drawing it on your paper.

As you go through this next meditation visualize it happening. Switch on your music and relax…. Go s-l-o-w-l-y.

Guided Meditation for your Vital Vision™ Blueprint. When you are sitting comfortably, hands in your lap and feet flat on the ground, without shoes, eyes closed, relaxed and focused on your breath, meditate with the intention to design the life you really want.

As you relax through your body from the top of your head, letting go, down through your forehead, face, nose, mouth and chin, letting go. Relax down through your neck and shoulders, feeling your arms heavy, relaxing down through your spine, your bottom, and feeling your legs heavy, and feet and toes heavy.

It's as if roots are growing out of your feet and going down into the earth, way, way down, as you connect yourself deeply with the earth's spinning core, fiery flames of lava bubbling red.

You notice a bright beautiful golden glow which weaves a golden thread to you through your feet, rising with you and through you as you rise back up through the earth.

The golden thread rising through your whole body, gently warming and energizing you, emerging from the top of your head and drawing you higher and higher as you see and feel yourself rising high into the sky, up above the clouds, through the atmosphere and up close in the darkness among the shining stars, connecting with and suspended in the time and space of the whole deep Universe.

As you are quietly and safely suspended there, you look down, way, way down, upon the beautiful earth you can see below your feet. The earth glows green and blue and you see a shining aura surrounding it. As you look you notice how wonderful the world is and how fortunate you are to be able to live there.

You notice that up where you are, you can see as a Creator. You have joined the Creator. You ARE the Creator - of your new life and your world!

You begin to rediscover your own Inner Vision and all that is in it.

See, with your eyes still closed, visualise yourself for who you are, moving forward, now that you are the Creator of Your New Life. Awaken your imagination and engage your intuition. See yourself happy and busy already drawing your Blueprint for your new life and knowing exactly who and what is in it and where you are.

See and remember how important to you this is. Remember all that you are capable of bringing in to yourself and giving back to this wonderful world, this earth, as you descend back slowly through the stratosphere, into the atmosphere, down through the clouds, down through the sky, slowly back into the room, seated in the room, ready to work with your materials and do your best work ever on your Vital Vision™ Blueprint.

When you are ready, slowly open your eyes and take in your surroundings, as you do so remember all that has just happened and the elements of your Vision and now begin your work.

"COURAGE Change is the ONLY way to Be, Do, Have More! Lead that Change! Never, Ever Give Up on Your Dreams "

Let's go then!

Emphatically NO TALKING while you create your Blueprint, you want to quieten your Inner Critic. Only after, when you feel your Blueprint is complete, is the time to SPEAK it out, record it and write down the elements of the Blueprint in the order you created them ready to Stormproof Your Success Strategies™ and Manifest Your Magnificent Masterplan™- all that you need to step out on your new journey into your new life.

Before you begin to create your Vital Vision™ Blueprint take a pause. Take a few deep breaths. Drink a glass of water.

NOW BEGIN. DRAW the most important picture you have ever drawn… Remember what you have seen, as the Creator. The Vision that you know in your heart is within….

Select as much paper as you need to create your Vital Vision™ Blueprint. Stand and look at that paper for a moment and realise what a wonderful opportunity you are facing - to start from a clean sheet and create whatever you want in your life from now forward. Breathe.

Begin when you are ready. Work mindfully. Be in the moment. Imagine you have permission to Be, Do and Have all that you really want. Listen intently to the music you are playing and focus on the music. Choose the colour of the pens you use thoughtfully, one at a time. Smell the beautiful aroma from your scented candle.

DO NOT SIT DOWN! Walk around the table while you work, seeing your BIG Picture from every angle and noticing the detail and being aware of what may still need to be included there…

YOU are the Creator of Your Life, including everything you allow into it. This is your opportunity to re-create what you want to draw to you.

Once you set this complete process in motion your brain's SuccessSATNAV™ will activate your subconscious and conscious to achieve your Vision. Remember that you cannot separate your life into business or personal when creating your holistic vision, simply because everything connects. That is the way of the world and the Universe.

What you do in your life impacts your business and vice versa. As it does for family, friends, clients and people you connect with. So be aware of this.

IMAGINE you are looking at a point in time, a date that you yourself want to set, in your future. The timescale is yours to decide. What have you always wanted to do, be and have but something always stopped you?

Dare to DREAM BIG because everything is Possible. The Universe shifts for what you want.

This is the time to be POSITIVE and very specific about who you want to be, what you want to DO and to have. You will achieve what you truly BELIEVE in.

Remember what you have just seen about your new life and draw it. Who are you? Where are you? What do you see around you? What do your surroundings look like? Introduce every aspect: you, your life, your achievements. If there's a role you play, for example a speaker, try it on in your imagination.

See yourself and whatever type of event you want, see your audience, who they are, how many. See what you are talking about. See them smiling and hear them clapping! Run through your presentation. You are not only your own life and world creator, but you are your own internal film producer too. Aren't you just amazing!

What are you wearing? What do you 'do'? Who is around you,

family, friends, colleagues, staff, the whole picture? What does your home look like? What car do you drive? Where are you holidaying? Are you working for others or are they working for you?

What great successes have you achieved as a result of the journey you are stepping onto today? Be absolutely clear and specific in the detail

This is ALL ABOUT YOU! And all that is in your world

Only once you are truly satisfied that you have given all that's necessary to this stage, we move on. To do that, double check again if needed. If this were your very last chance to make sure everything you want to attract into your vision is there, is it? Look again! Something you are unsure about? Go On! Put it in!

Finished? Then Sign your work and take a photograph.

Take a five-minute break, have a drink of water or cup of coffee.

Now is the time for words….

Look at your Blueprint now. Speak out aloud as you write down, and record, how you would describe every single element in your Vital Vision™ to me or to anyone else.

Be as clear and detailed as you can. This is also embedding into your subconscious.

Start with where you began drawing and explain what you have drawn, moving on to the next part, and the next, and the next until you have spoken about, written down and recoded every element of your Blueprint and how each element interacts with the others and all the connections in there to who, where and how you want your life to be.

Something truly magical has now happened. Your Subconscious SuccessSATNAV™ has clocked your destination, route-mapped your journey and you are already on your way!

Suddenly, all the opportunities for you to achieve this new life (that are already there, hidden in plain sight but you were not attuned into their wavelength) will start showing up, and you will automatically know which ones are right for you. And the beauty is this is working for you 24/7 and 365 even when you are not thinking about it!

Display your Blueprint in a prominent place where you will see it every day. As time passes, feel free to add anything to it and when parts of it are achieved, as they will be, Celebrate!

Do not be at all surprised if something BIG and totally unexpected appeared in your Vital Vision™ Blueprint.

This has happened for every client I have worked with! For example, the urge to speak on global stages and write and publish a book in less than 90 days, which was launched by Michele Walsh, and entitled The BIG Shift!.

To start a new national charity helping children who are victims of domestic violence and abuse as did Karen Williams founder of The Buddy Bag Foundation.

To launch her existing beautiful book "Little Chick Has Lunch on the Moon" together with her new "Dreams Workshops" for schools to a global marketplace from South Africa, as did Alison Delaney.

To set up a global Wealth Building Academy of Excellence, that will benefit deprived and disadvantaged young people which is now in progress with Chris J Henry and much more.

Whatever it is and however outrageous (or not) it may seem, it is meant to be. Trust it! It usually relates to a Higher Purpose hidden within you, and comes from your Heart, Mind, Body and Spirit reconnection that happened as a natural part of this process.

You may not yet understand this but it is meant to be, and will become much clearer in a short space of time when people and resources that relate to this being manifested are attracted to you or brought into your attention.

From the words you used to describe your vision, or from the Blueprint itself, words will have emerged that lead you to your purpose, your why!

You can create from these a statement for your Vision, a Statement for your Why or Purpose and your statement for your Mission (what you are going to do to achieve your vision).

These single sentences or phrases are a quick way to inspire and motivate you and make it easier for other people, supporters especially, to grasp.

Including these in a paragraph will enable you to describe your whole vision and enable others to see your bigger picture.

Here's the beautiful part though. You can see your bigger picture too. Not only this but you also have the power of your complete vision inside of you, to inspire, motivate and move you, pull you forward. Much more enjoyable than being pushed there by the pain of uncertainty!

Remember to check in with your Values too.

And pictures…..

Visualise your Vital Vision™

Yes, you know what is in your Vital Vision™ Blueprint in every little detail. Continue to look at it every day. Revisit it often in your mind's eye too to bring it alive.

Play with it and have fun! Your mind cannot distinguish between what is real and what you are imagining. This is a proven scientific fact! And the more you see what's in there, the closer it will come.

If there's a particular car, see yourself in that car, in that make and model of that car, the colour, the car registration number, the fuel.

Smell the new interior leather. See yourself driving it and observe every little detail. Better still, book a test drive and get a real feel for it! If there's a boat, use same process and that goes for everything in your vision! Live it and breathe it!

Blueprints are created for all sorts of purposes. Architects, Designers, Innovators, all are creators of blueprints, then models and structures. It's not so usual to create the blueprint for your own life, so WELL DONE!

And a timely remember that you cannot work against your values as I have said before, or with people who do not share your Values. So, check them again against the list you compiled from the chapter on **Values**.

Do not be concerned if you feel you cannot figure anything out. Know this. The Magic! has now already happened and you are on your way to your Wonderful Life.

Now Get ready to Stormproof Your Success Strategies™

Congratulations! Major Achievement Alert!

Well Done You!

"Be Thankful For What You Have, You'll End Up Having More"

Oprah

Chapter Nine

STEP 5 STORMPROOF YOUR SUCCESS STRATEGIES

Stormproof Your Success Strategies™ now, and you are also preparing for your next step, Manifest Your Magnificent Masterplan™!

Now you have looked at your **Who**, your **Why?** and your **Vision** it is time to look at **What and How** you achieve the elements of your Vital Vision™ Blueprint, and in what priority. The choices are all yours. (Remember that your subconscious is on side now helping you too!)

Again, for this chapter and this exercise, remember to meditate first and then TAKE YOUR TIME! It will be worth it.

One Rule: Everything goes, no matter how silly the idea seems at this stage. Think also and note down every possible thought you have about what is in your vision and what can impact it either negatively or positively, internally or externally, by you or other people. As with the weather, if a storm is possible you'd best be prepared!

Don't overthink though. Once a thought comes in jot it down on a sticky note! Capture it in the moment or it may be gone forever! Whatever that thought or idea is you will find a place for it, whether it eventually needs action or not!

Once you have all the ideas, then is the time to go through and see which ones are practical or achievable or even possible, on your own or with the right help. You are looking for quantity of ideas at this stage....

To give you an example, if writing a book is in your vision, then what needs to be done to make that happen? What are the steps? Do you have the resources, or do you need to obtain them? Who do you know who could help? What do you know that could help? Where could you go for help? What is the book about? You can stormproof that too.

Stormproofing is just like Brainstorming ideas except taking things a little further - setting yourself up for Success.

Time to Name and Shame Your Obstacles and Befriend Your Resources!

You intend to make this Vital Vision™ Unstoppable! So, in this session you will **Name and Shame Your Obstacles**. Exactly that! What can get in the way of you achieving your vision for your new life? Identify those people, (including yourself!), organisations, skills, qualities, resource issues, whatever else, can sabotage success. Think about your Values too!

Obstacles are the **Weaknesses** (internal) that you yourself, or your dreams and plans have, including skills, experience, resources, connections, funding, whatever and the **Threats** (external) that others may use that would derail your vision.

This could be anything from family, friends, communities, cultures, funders, governments or more. Forewarned is forearmed and you can then design appropriate strategies to plan, find allies and advocates, then overcome and succeed.

You also **Befriend Your Resources - Strengths and Opportunities,** many of which are so easily overlooked. These may be particular, skills, experiences, talents, gifts, knowledge, learnings, group or organisational memberships, networks, products (even those you are currently doing nothing with) people who are potentially great Advocates or Champions for you and your mission or present the right level of Challenge and Accountability to keep you on course.

You also identify which **Weaknesses** and **Threats** that, with your own or other people's intervention, can in reality be turned into **Opportunities!** As an example a talent, skill or product you have been sitting on but you not promoting may be a weakness that with the right promotion may be a huge opportunity you are missing - if the timing is now right!

Time to Name and Shame Your Obstacles and Befriend Your Resources!

So, let's look at this a different way!

Take a large sheet of paper, Flip Chart size as a minimum, or even a roll of paper, choosing the size you want to work with. Divide it into 4 sections headed with a marker pen into Strengths, Weaknesses, Opportunities and Threats.

Blue tack or sticky tape this onto a wall preferably, though you can work on a flat surface. Being able to stand back and see the bigger picture is especially useful.

Then have four different coloured sticky notes pads. For example:

Red for Threats

Green for Strengths

Yellow for Opportunities

Blue for Weaknesses

Do not worry about getting your thoughts into the right sections at this stage. Do not let anything slow you down or stop you.

Don't overthink. While the thought is in your mind just get it down onto paper quickly, to make room for more thoughts to come out. If it is easy to post your note in the right section straight away, do it. If not post it in a space at the side to look at again when you have finished.

Sometimes it's not really clear which section a thought goes into. So, as you identify a strength, threat, weakness or opportunity, write on the relevant colour sticky note and attach it to the larger sheet of paper.

If you can put it straight into the right section, do so now. When you are finished with stormproofing thoughts and ideas you will check that they are all arranged under either Strengths, Weaknesses, Opportunities or Threats.

To make this even more interesting you will then organize these thoughts and ideas into topics that form the basis of your Masterplan.

You can use different coloured pens to organize so that for example you could choose a red marker to indicate a Marketing Idea and a Blue marker to indicate a Systems Idea as follows:

Opportunities on a yellow sticky note that are for Marketing will have a red dot marked on them. Opportunities for systems, on a yellow note, are marked with a blue dot.

Likewise, Strengths written on green sticky notes will have a red dot for Marketing then Strengths in systems are marked with blue marker pen.

You get the idea.

Where the value lies here is at the end of your stormproofing you have already colour coded your strategic areas for action that are related. For example, you'll see your Marketing Strengths, Opportunities, Weaknesses and Threats sticky notes all have a dot in red marker and give you a focus for YOUR Marketing Plan. All those written in blue give you a focus for your Systems, and so on!

Ultimately, you decide which are to be actioned and the order of priorities as strategies here and in your Masterplan going forward.

So, then create main new headings on a very large sheet or roll of paper for the two key aspects of your Vision, Personal Life and Business Life, then rearrange the relevant sticky notes into key topics or themes under these for action in your Masterplan.

For example, one key heading is Personal Life, which includes family and other personal areas for action, holidays perhaps if they feature as key in your vision, hobbies, new learning, friends and relationships and so on. Whatever has come up with issues at this part of the process that will need to be dealt with in some way to ensure a successful outcome.

The other key heading is for Business Life which would likely include sticky notes for Finances, Systems, Marketing, Sales, Clients, Products, Programme Development and so on.

Again, this is about whatever has come up in this session, on those topics, that will need some action to ensure a successful outcome in creating the life and business that you love!

Eventually, you have transferred all the elements in your Vision onto your Stormproofing Charts and assessed them in terms of Strengths, Weaknesses, Opportunities and Threats to achieving your vision.

You have then further organized them into themes and identified which you want or need to take action on, ordered with priorities first.

You may want to take a break at this stage before moving on or you may be so close you want to continue.

The timing of the whole process of this book is completely down to you. It is your life after all!

The process described above, as used in the Destination Me™ programme and which has rave reviews from clients, is specifically designed to be extensive, to capture more ideas, to secure much more detail than a traditional S.W.O.T., and arranged so that much of the work is already done for you, now you are ready to Manifest Your Magnificent MasterPlan™

Now get ready to make your final choices from this session, the elements that you love and want to be part of your future that you are going to schedule and take action on. The choices are always yours.

The traditional S.W.O.T Format with which you may be familiar is shown below.

Strengths (Internal)	Weaknesses (Internal)
Opportunities (External)	Threats (External)

So now, we are almost there! Do the following exercises then let's Go Forward, into your Magnificent Masterplan.

Stormproof Your Success Strategies Exercise 1a.

What 3 Key Strengths have you become more aware of as a result of Stormproof Your Success Strategies?

1.

_____

_____

_____

2.

_____

_____

_____

3.

_____

_____

_____

_____

Stormproof Your Success Strategies Exercise 1b.

What Action do you intend to take to build on or leverage your 3 Key Strengths?

1.

2.

3.

Stormproof Your Success Strategies Exercise 2a.

What 3 Key Weaknesses have you become more aware of as a result of Stormproof Your Success Strategies?

1.

2.

3.

Stormproof Your Success Strategies Exercise 2b.

What Action do you intend to take on your 3 Key Weaknesses?

1.

_____

_____

_____

_____

2.

_____

_____

_____

3.

_____

_____

_____

Stormproof Your Success Strategies Exercise 3a.

What 3 Key Opportunities have you become more aware of as a result of Stormproof Your Success Strategies?

1.

_____

_____

_____

_____

2.

_____

_____

_____

3.

_____

_____

_____

_____

Stormproof Your Success Strategies Exercise 3b.

What action do you intend to take about your 3 Key Opportunities?

1.

_____

_____

_____

_____

2.

_____

_____

_____

3.

_____

_____

_____

Stormproof Your Success Strategies Exercise 4a.

What 3 Key Threats have you become more aware of as a result of Stormproof Your Success Strategies?

1.

_____

_____

_____

_____

_____

2.

_____

_____

_____

3.

_____

_____

_____

_____

Stormproof Your Success Strategies Exercise 4b.

What action, if any, can you or do you want or need to take on your 3 Key Threats

1.

2.

3.

Stormproof Your Success Strategies Exercise 5.

Overall, what is your most powerful discovery from this Chapter?

CONGRATULATIONS!

We Are Almost There!

Dream BIG and Aim HIGH!

Shine Your Light Brightly

For You Are Made of Stars!

And You Light Up Our Lives!

Chapter Ten

STEP 6 MANIFEST YOUR MAGNIFICENT MASTERPLAN FOR THE NEW YOU! AND TAKE RIGHT ACTION!

G o For It! Manifest Your Magnificent Masterplan™!

CONGRATULATIONS! Well Done for getting this far, especially if you have taken your time and studied each chapter.

Especially if you have meditated before each exercise and started meditating as a new habit, a daily routine, preferably in the morning to set you up for each day. In the evening, especially just before going to sleep, is good too, when you can set the intention for tomorrow to be A Wonderful Day!!

Now you have the result of your Stormproofing exercise, you can decide which are YOUR priorities for your life from all the work you have done throughout this particular journey that aligns with your Vital Vision™ Blueprint! Now you'll look a little closer at the **What** so that you can add the **Where, When and with Whom**

Now you can put these into words as well as images so that your conscious mind gets familiar with them.

You are now already 99% there!

So, what IS a Masterplan? I've heard it described as a Future

Vision and it is. Traditionally it is often for large scale operations and results in a very bulky written document.

Your Masterplan is simply the overarching document that tells you what you are going to do, where and when you'll do it, with whom and what resources you'll need. You can then set your calendar so that everything happens at the right time in the most important order to set you up for success.

The magical thing about a Masterplan for your life is for it to be a living, breathing thing, which is what you are achieving. You have already done the Magical bit by doing the inner work.

In this book you have worked through Who and Why you are, your Story, Mindset and Values, created your Vital Vision™ Blueprint and stormproofed your success!

If we were to have a conversation now, you are at the point where you should be able to tell me your vision without much thought and how it is going to be achieved.

This is already working inside of you through your subconscious SuccessSATNAV™ which is most definitely switched on!

However, when your vision affects other people and needs to get them involved, needs resources and has things that need time allocating, you need that overarching plan to pull it all together to ensure the right people know at the right times and resources are attracted and allocated.

As an example:

Say that a priority for Action is to have more free time for yourself or go on more exotic holidays. Then that part of your Masterplan is just like making a plan for the things you would do to ensure you have a fantastic holiday!

For this holiday you'll need to decide the timing, destination, method of travel, finances, insurance, who is going, what extras there are, for example, travel costs, specific clothing for environment) and arrive at the plan for that element. You'll also need to think about the steps you need to take and when, for example paying the deposit and following through with the final balance. If you've ever planned a holiday or even a road journey, you can do this. It's all common sense.

You can handwrite your masterplan or create it in a Word or other document and use Excel charts for some of it. Whatever works best for you. If you create it on the computer, do print out a copy.

I cannot over-emphasise the importance of getting your Masterplan onto paper in some shape or form because that has a physical effect! In the same way that bringing your vision out of you and into the world in a physical document has already had an effect.

And there is no right or wrong way! In the Destination Me™ programme we go through this process online together. For this book, you will do this any way it makes sense for you, as long as you do it!

If you need further help, email

valerie@mywonderfullifecoach.co.uk

Your masterplan can be as complicated or as simple as you wish to make it, as long or as short.

It could focus on one thing only and be written on a postcard or be a short plan of Action. Action being the important word.

What is important is to bring in your BIG PRIORITIES for Action from your vision and stormproofing sessions into a document so that you can identify the key players, apply timescales, commit resources and before you know it you'll arrive at:

ACTION, ACCOUNTABILITY, ACHIEVEMENT!

You have now done enough work to know Who you really are and Who you want to be.

You know Why? you are, Who you want to serve What you want in your life.

By now you will also have identified the How, Where and When.

If any of this is still not clear, time to reschedule, re-read and work again through this book, one Chapter at a time in the order as printed.

Whenever you arrive at this point in the book, provided you have completed all of the exercises, you have just taken the first set of 6 BIG STEPS that are your firm foundation.

Know that your journey is not over, it is just beginning. And a wonderful adventure it promises to be.

Set yourself s-t-r-e-t-c-h-i-n-g Goals as part of your Masterplan. You set the timeframe to match your Vision. 5 years? 3 Years? One Year?

Then, having started with the end in sight (your Vision), work back in your mind to this moment, here and now, for the first Next Steps you need to take. A good starting point is to set yourself your first 90 Day Plan, breaking this down into elements required for each goal and dividing this into the weeks leading up to your 90 Days, working on a maximum of four Goals.

One of these goals will be the BIG Purpose that dominates your Vision. Now you have found it, and the Universe attracts what you need, be ready to take RIGHT ACTION to make it happen.

"Set A Goal SO BIG That You Can't Achieve It Until YOU GROW INTO THE PERSON THAT CAN"

Author Unknown

Remember to continue with your Daily habits:

- Look at., speak and move to your Affirmations and Mantras
- Be alert to and explore opportunities the Universe attracts
- Be conscious of your Mindset, negatives repel what you want and positives attract all that is in your vision
- Meditate
- Closely look at your Vital Vision™ Blueprint
- Visualise your Vision happening in your mind's eye
- Look after your health too - exercise, eat good food
- Take Action on at least one Goal from your Masterplan
- Keep up your Gratitude Journal

Set up weekly habits:

o Review your Masterplan once a week. Is what you do each day moving you closer towards your Goals and Vision? If yes, its all good. If no, what do you need to tweak or adapt?

Nothing can happen without ACTION! and nothing works unless you do!

You now have the Universe on your side and you will attract what you need but when you do, it is you who will make it happen by taking up those opportunities.

Be confident and brave to take whatever steps you need to have the reward of living the life you love.

You will notice a change in yourself and in how people perceive you.

Stride forward, shoulders back, head high, smile on your face. You now know the power of you. Don't hide from it. Share it with the world by living the life you were born to lead!

The secret other 1% or is it 100%? Your subconscious SuccessSATNAV™ is working on your Vision for you 24/7 and 365!

One Client described this as The Law of Attraction, The Secret and Cosmic Ordering on steroids - with Rocket Fuel added!

Having reached this far, worked through each and every Step AND done all the exercises in the right order

Know this! You Already Now Have ALL You Need To Succeed!

Now commit to birthing your Vital Vision Blueprint into the world and Make it Happen by taking
RIGHT ACTION!

You've Got This! No Matter What!
But! In case you are in any doubt whatsoever, I have a couple of final thoughts and exercises for you!

Exercise 1.

If I discovered that I had just one week left to live, I would most definitely:

1.

_____

_____

_____

_____

2.

_____

_____

_____

_____

3.

_____

_____

_____

_____

Some hints:

My life

My Bucket List

My legacy

My family

My business

My book

My programme

My CORE Message

Exercise 2.

For myself, each of my seven days I would:

1.

2.

3.

4.

5.

_____

_____

_____

6.

_____

_____

_____

7.

_____

_____

_____

My question now is: Why Wait Until It is Too Late?

Get on with it and start Living Your Legacy Today.

You are a miracle, unique and here for your purpose.

The world needs you NOW.

So, don't wait a minute longer!

Whatever you have burning inside of you to share with the world, whether it is one person at a time or one to many - Get on with it!

Don't leave this place with your song still unsung!

Otherwise, no one will ever know!

A Journey of One Thousand Miles
Begins with a Single Step

Lao Tzu

Appendix 1

Environment Checklist for All Your Steps

Here is your handy Checklist as a reminder of what is needed to prepare:

REMEMBER: - You are on the journey to YOUR MOST IMPORTANT WORK so do this for as long as it takes until you feel ready to move on... Do not rush this.

1. Time and Timing: -

Your Session length varies according to your needs, the amount of mind and/or physical 'baggage' you need to clear and the size of your ambition. You are on the journey to YOUR MOST IMPORTANT WORK so do this for as long as it takes until you feel ready to move on...

Date Booked in the diary for your Steps	☐
Allow a whole day, Me Time, each time although the exercises may take you less	☐
Book some time for Physical Decluttering beforehand too	☐
Advise people in advance that you will not be reachable on these dates	☐
Arrange to take care of any pressing business beforehand	☐

2. Room or Location:-

Consider carefully WHERE to take your Steps that:

Inspires you	☐
Is quiet and calming	☐
Is uncluttered	☐
Has Temperature exactly right	☐
Draws Natural daylight by preference	☐
Has comfortable seating and table/desk	☐
Has Access to power/equipment for your meditation/music	☐
Has convenient supply of filtered water	☐
Ensures that sounds will not disturb others	☐
There will be no external noises to distract you	☐
Is a place where you will have no interruptions	☐
You have cancelled all calls/loose/casual clothing and footwear	☐
Atmosphere:-	☐
Check you have sourced and purchased your favourite fragranced Candle to use when you are ready to begin your meditation	☐
Check that it will be safe to use in the environment you have chosen	☐

Appendix 2

Materials and Resources Checklist – Your Core Materials:

Flip Chart Pad, OR roll of white or coloured paper or a4 sheets	☐
If A4 sheets used, have also a roll of sticky tape plus Blue-tack	☐
Notebook and pen	☐
Selection of coloured markers or coloured crayons, pens, or pencils	☐
4 different colour pads of sticky notes	☐
Music player	☐
Video/still Camera on any device	☐
Fragranced Candle or Incense Burner	☐
Check sound level from your computer or equipment speakers can be adjusted	☐
Comfortable Chair and Desk or Table	☐

The Thing About Comfort Zone is This! Once You Firmly Decide to Step Outside, After the Initial Fear, Comes Excitement, Exhilaration Success. Keep Going! Never, Ever Give Up On Your #Dreams!

ABOUT THE AUTHOR

Valerie Dwyer is a Best Seller Author, Award-Winning Entrepreneur, Inspirational Speaker and Overcomer of Challenges!.

She is the founder of My Wonderful Life Coach™, a leading entrepreneur coaching and mentoring practice specialising in Vision, Strategy and Confidence Building, with clients in the UK, Europe, Australia, New Zealand, US, Canada and Indonesia.

My Wonderful Life Coach's vision is to empower and enable entrepreneurs through their own individual or corporate shared visions to create a better, more sustainable, healthy and harmonious world while reinventing their own lives and businesses to be more on purpose, fulfilled, abundant and successful, in whatever way success means to them.

Valerie founded her first business aged eighteen and has gone on to start, buy, merge, grow and sell ten business, from sole operators to partnerships and limited companies, employing people and creating opportunities for many to begin their own start-ups.

The transformational holistic Destination Me™ programme she has developed that aligns the Heart, Mind, Body and Spirit with Vision, Values and Strategies has raving fan clients and referral rates are high.

The combined knowledge and gifts of over thirty years' experience of starting, growing and reinventing businesses; surviving and thriving through three recessions, downturns and economic collapse plus overcoming the physical and mental chaos of life threatening situations informs the impactfulness of this programme which is now in development as a powerful toolkit for coaches, mentors and facilitators to deliver in their own client programmes.

Experiencing for herself that the saying "when you hit rock bottom the only way is up" is easier said than done, she shares what she has learned as the Grand Master in the art of creative reinvention and empowers entrepreneurs with these skills by taking them right back to basics, giving them a clean sheet plus the tools and techniques to create a powerful and unshakeable inner foundation for designing and living the new life of their dreams.

Recognised by the UK Government as a Champion for Women's Enterprise as a Member of the Women's Enterprise Taskforce and an invited guest of HRH Queen Elizabeth II at no less than three Royal Garden Parties, Valerie is a well-regarded international speaker on women, enterprise and leadership appearing on radio, television and at major conferences. She has been referenced by leading publications and featured in and contributed to several other author's books.

Valerie is a former President, Chairman, Non-Exec Director, Managing Director and Board Member of several businesses, organisations and charities. She is a philanthropist who gives back in many ways in gratitude for her success, including as a Lifetime Global Partner of B1G1, funding local worthy causes around the world that align with the UN Sustainable Development Goals.

Oh! And thanks to her Mentor Andy Harrington, she overcame the fear of breaking her left wrist a second time to learn in three minutes to successfully karate chop and break through a solid 1-inch thick block of wood! #Mindset!

Valerie wrote this book after undergoing three operations to save the eyesight in her left eye. Though apparently stabilised, it has left her with poor eyesight that made this task another challenge to overcome!

Connect with Valerie for Q&A, to give feedback and request further resources by email valerie@mywonderfullifecoach.co.uk

What Clients say:

"I had the pleasure of spending a fabulous day with Valerie going through her Vital Vision process. It was brilliant! Each part of the day was carefully balanced to ensure that I got maximum benefit and clarity from our time together. I would highly recommend to any entrepreneur looking for deeper clarity of vision and direction. xx"

Bernadette Sarginson, Empower Coaching and Training

Within a short time of creating her Vital Vision™ Success Blueprint, Alison had the Global Launch of her 'Little Bird Dreams Workshops' from South Africa and then Founded 'Rise Up' Coach.

In her Video Testimonial Alison talks about how Powerful the Vital Vision™ Blueprint session was for her, and how she was able to open up her creative mind space using 'Clear Your Mind Clutter' in order to be fully in the state to Design the Life and Business She Loves. I treasure her words "Thank You Valerie xxx"

Alison Delaney, Founder of Little Bird People Development, Coach, Author of 'Little Chick Has Lunch on the Moon'.

Since her Vital Vision™ Success Blueprint, Karen Williams Founded The Buddy Bag Foundation UK, Making a Difference to Children in Emergency Care– beating ALL targets and now a member of B1G1 global worthy causes. Upcoming Author and WINNER of a number of accolades including Networker of The Year 2018.

"I was at a crossroads in my life! I had worked with Valerie in a previous life and had always been inspired by Valerie's vision, enthusiasm and integrity. After a one to one session with Valerie I embarked on a Vital Vision™ visualization workshop with her that was extremely powerful and enlightening! I do believe that when you visualize you materialise your goals and dreams. Valerie however took me on a journey out of my Comfort Zone!

But I left the Universe with belief and it delivered! My business has grown and I have helped 1000's of people save money and make money and so much more achieved! Thank You Valerie xx"

Karen Williams Founder, the Buddy Bag Foundation, Successful Entrepreneur, High Level Network Marketing Professional, Trainer and Speaker

After only our first session Michele said – "Hi Valerie. Just a quick email whilst I catch my breath. I have been full on manifesting and creating paths to my new Vital Vision™ like you wouldn't believe. Business is 'going through the roof'. I barely have time to sleep but I can do that on the plane. Going great guns and definitely feel like I've had Rocket Fuel up my rear end! Let the Good Times roll and roll. Thank You Valerie xxx"

Michele Walsh, Business Coach, Author, Speaker. Since her Vital Vision™ Success Blueprint, the Creator of 'Dream Believe Attract' and Best-Selling Author of The BIG Shift.

"Valerie one big thank you for YOU are the ANGEL sent to get me out there! As you are with all women who desire to take the STAGE and SHINE I feel the newness too, so much and yes the Native Retreat was food for thought very much so.

Just wanted to say thank you so much for a great day yesterday, the Vital Vision™ process is amazing Valerie. What a powerful day! I have had a lot of light bulb moments that have been miracles. What is interesting is I broke through at the weekend, not so much with clients but within myself.

It has been a radical transformation and I was given lots of information about my niche and purpose I do feel this is due to you and what needed to come through, Thank you so much. Wow what a journey!"

I feel I am back in and on track after years out big time. Thank You Valerie xxxxxx"

Julie Anne Hart, International Intuitive and Leadership Expert Since her Vital Vision™ Success Blueprint, the Founder of Wise Women Global, Wise Women Academy and other 'Firsts.

After only one week Chrissy White: Vibrant Gourmet – and Speaker "These last days (and evenings) have been so full and interesting, not to mention exciting, especially in terms of my BIG VISION. My vision is really landing in my body and my reality and I am starting to activate my Vital Vision™ Success Blueprint. Thank you hugely Valerie for being in my life and creating all new possibilities xx"

Chrissy White, Founder, Vibrant Gourmet. Since her Vital Vision™ Success Blueprint – Launched her 'Goddess Gatherings'

After our session Sue Ritchie said: "I just wanted to thank you for the Business Breakthrough session. I came to the session feeling a little lost and lacking clarity of where I should be taking things. The process you took me through was very powerful. I liked your approach which was very supportive, and encouraging, but at the same time you didn't let me off the hook, which was just what I needed. I left the session feeling excited and with a clear action plan.

Valerie is Amazing. In just a couple of hours doing a 'Vital Vision™ Business Breakthrough Session' that also tackled some limiting beliefs holding me back, I had my breakthrough! Powerful! I also want to Thank You for your insights and advice. It has been really helpful in clarifying my thoughts. I really appreciate your help". Thank You Valerie xxx".

Sue Ritchie, Your Ecstatic Health, Wellness Coach and Mentor, Speaker. Since her Vital Vision Business Breakthrough Session – Sue is the Author of 'Love Your Gut'.

"Valerie has assisted me with Visioning for me and my business. She is the Perfect Coach and Mentor to help You take your business forward. I cannot speak highly enough of her!"

Bettina Yarde, MD Morgan Dias. Legal Professional Firm. Since her Vital Vision Business Breakthrough Session – Bettina became a Legal Expert on Sky Legal TV, invited to a Reception in the Houses of Parliament; Launched a Corporate Programme; Grew her business and was recognised as a Finalist in 3 major Entrepreneurial Awards including prestigious UK Women of The Future.

Valerie Mentored Tasneem Dakri through the Idea to Enterprise Programme where Valerie had been a Speaker and also delivered the powerful Vital Vision Blueprint™ WorkshopTasneem said: "Valerie has been a wonderful coach. She inspired me and built my confidence, she easily highlighted areas where I could concentrate on more in terms of becoming successful. I really enjoyed working with Valerie as she is talented in many areas of business and has a wide range of skills that certainly helped with furthering the success of my venture.

Valerie is accomplished, approachable and a has a very positive outlook which makes her a superb mentor. I am very pleased to have met Valerie as I know I will always have a strong-minded businesswoman to take inspiration from". Thank you, Valerie x"

Tasneem Dakri, V:GD Desserts

"Brilliant lady – pushed me hard to make me think but also encouraged me and was very positive. I wasn't sure what to expect so I didn't have particular expectations – I thought we'd be going through business plans but the sessions went deeper than that and took me back to basics and my vision – which is what I actually needed – although I didn't realise that at first!

This was very useful and helped me to focus on what I want to do, develop my vision and start to research and plan out new services. Valerie also provided me with excellent resources that she'd developed and uses as part of her mentoring/coaching."

Sue Mitchell, Bluebell Business Services

"I was introduced to Valerie as part of the Idea to Enterprise Programme, supporting Women in Business and was pleased to have some support sessions from her.

Valerie helped me to set out a new Vision for my business and think through what I really loved to do. "What floats your boat?" was a key phrase! That then became a huge change and turn around in my business model. As a result of those sessions I now have a business I feel is much more "me". I help other women in business reduce their stress by being more organised and effective. This clears their heads and helps their business to grow. Valerie was instrumental at kicking off a new business model for me and I'm very grateful to her!"

Sue Grogan, Joined Up Work - Life & Work Organiser

CASE STUDY

Karen Williams, Successful, Award-winning Entrepreneur, Speaker, Founder of The Buddy Bag Foundation - Making A Difference to Children in Emergency Care

Karen and I have known each other and worked together on successful business projects for several years in our different enterprises.

Then after an all-change for Karen, from selling her then business and starting out afresh, she chose to go through the holistic Destination Me™ Vital Vision™ Blueprint process to design her ideal future with me at My Wonderful Life Coach™ for the first time.

Within a couple of years Karen had achieved everything in that Vision including overcoming her fears to become a recognised and well received motivational public speaker.

So, Karen came back again, ready to go through the experience again to move onwards and upwards with an even more ambitious Vision. The process repeated and Karen went on to achieve all the goals she had set herself, related to her Vision.

In 2013 Karen got in tune with her continually stretching Inner Vision and this time there was something detailed in there that we neither had any idea what it was about. It was a Foundation! That's it. A Foundation!

This was then a mystery to both of us. We talked around the idea of it maybe being a Charity but that was it. It was by no means the main focus of that iteration of Karen's Vision but then in 2014 something really interesting happened.

Karen had been on holiday and visiting family in Australia when she came across the Allanah and Madeleine Foundation and the Buddy Bag Foundation idea was sown. In 2015 the very first Buddy Bag pack took place in Staffordshire, UK., and in the same year the Foundation officially became a Registered Charity.

Then…. in 2017, through a chance meeting in Bali with Paul Dunn, Chairman of B1G1, the Global Giving Initiative founded by Masami Sato, my business became a Lifetime Global Partner of B1G1, Business For Good, the Global Giving Initiative.

During one conversations with Karen about her then Vision I happened to say "Wouldn't it be Wonderful if the Buddy Bag Foundation could be recognised as a worthy cause by B1G1 and able to receive global funding to support this valuable work?"

We checked what was necessary to qualify and the first hurdle was the requirement for sets of accounts covering 3 years, as a registered charity. This then set a minimum time frame as goal by which to qualify. Then we talked about how to measure, demonstrate and communicate the impacts the Buddy Bag Foundation was making across the UK.

One thing led to another and I saw Karen take the Buddy Bag Foundation past the first set of goals ahead of target, then ahead of the revised target and then ahead of another revised target, so that the original goal of 200 Buddy Bags sourced, packed and delivered by 2020 went from 200 to 2,000 and up to 20,000 and now they have achieved over 26,000!

This may not seem a lot to many but comforting, supporting and positively impacting in the process the lives of 26,000 children in emergency care, and their mothers, removed from their homes through domestic abuse. That is some ask! Especially when you see the contents of each individual Buddy Bag that needs to be sourced, packed and delivered at no cost to the organisation!

Karen has done something amazing! Across the UK She has built a Board, a Team, Advisers, an army of Volunteers, Angels, Sponsors and Supporters. The Buddy Bag Foundation even has its own official Guide Badge! Buddy bag Foundation Challenge Badge and Buddy the Teddy Bear!

But more than this, The Buddy Bag Foundation has provided comfort and inspiration to children and their mothers throughout the UK, in difficult, often traumatic domestic situations, as well as providing valuable cohesive structured team building and Corporate Social Responsibility initiatives for companies of all sizes.

Karen has been able to maintain her commitment that 100% of

all funds raised goes directly to the charity through the generosity of the many supporters who continue to contribute to this essential work.

When Good…Then Good….

I am delighted to announce that for everyone who commits to creating their ideal life and signs up to join the transformational and experiential Destination Me™ Intensive online programme, through our Lifetime Global Partnership with B1G1, the Giving Initiative, we will gift a fully packed Buddy Bag on your behalf to a child in emergency care in the UK as a result of domestic violence or abuse.

Go here to join the waitlist and I look forward to seeing you on the inside

https://www.mywonderfullifecoach.co.uk/destination-me/

Find out more at **https://www.buddybagfoundation.co.uk**

More about B1G1 at **https://www.b1g1.com**

Glossary of Terms

Destination Me™ Intensive

A 6 week holistic transformational VIP programme containing the 6 Steps to Reinvent Your Life that takes you from stuck to success. Delivered with you - offline and online.

My Wonderful Life Coach™

The lead Coaching and Mentoring organisation that developed, delivers and licenses the Destination Me™ Intensive programme

Guided Meditation

Within the context of this book and the Destination Me™ Intensive programme, meditation that includes more than calm, peaceful, relaxing musing and/or music. In this case, powerful spoken guidance, either with or without music to enable clear and specific visualisations and experiences.

Kundalini Awakening

The closest description we have found is:

"Kundalini is your life force energy. It's believed that in those who are unawakened, their energy remains coiled at the base of their spine. For those who have an awakening event and become conscious, the energy spirals upward, activating each chakra, and making the being transition into an enlightened guru".

Shaman

A *shaman*, is believed to interact with a spirit world through altered states of consciousness, such as trance. The goal is usually to direct these spirits or spiritual energies into the physical world, for healing or some other desired purpose.

My Thank You - To You!

Thank you again for buying and reading this book, and more importantly, committing to work through the 6 Steps to Reinvent Your Life, to go for the life you REALLY want!

I hope you have enjoyed working through the programme and have been rewarded with the learning and insights it brings.

I appreciate You and I would Love Your Feedback! Email: valerie@mywonderfullifecoach.co.uk

Thank you that you have contributed to training for new entrepreneurs in less fortunate countries, access to education and reading materials for young girls, fruit trees as sources of food and income to sustain impoverished families plus fresh, life-saving water for families who need it. All gifted through the Lifetime Global Partnership between B1G1 and My Wonderful Life Coach™ **Thank you!**

Share your Vision, get it out into the world in a bigger way, feel free to share with me too! I would especially love to see you on the programme if you'd like to experience your journey to the next level.

We love what we do and we'd like you to be part of our community of entrepreneurs who are creating the life and business of their dreams.

To hear about special events, updates, new books, receive personal invitations, access resources and keep in touch, go register on the Destination Me™ page and we'll see you inside:

https://www.mywonderfullifecoach.co.uk/destination-me/

We'd love you to rate this book and write a review on Amazon too.

Here's to YOU! Living the Life you Love!
Valerie Dwyer, Founder, My Wonderful Life Coach™

Courage Tiger!

See How You Have Grown!

You've Definitely Got This!

No Matter What!

FINALLY!

From time to time we develop new programmes, workshops, talks, books, projects, with opportunities to join in beta tests, trials, readings, reviews.
Our community, and private Facebook Group are the first to hear about these opportunities, so we look forward to seeing you there

https://www.mywonderfullifecoach.co.uk/destination-me/

Printed in Poland
by Amazon Fulfillment
Poland Sp. z o.o., Wrocław

63274842R00132